D0481646

Think, Act, and
Invest Like
Warren Buffett

Think, Act, and Invest Like Warren Buffett

THE WINNING STRATEGY TO HELP YOU ACHIEVE YOUR FINANCIAL AND LIFE GOALS

Larry E. Swedroe

Illustrations by Carl Richards

NEW YORK   CHICAGO   SAN FRANCISCO
LISBON   LONDON   MADRID   MEXICO CITY   MILAN
NEW DELHI   SAN JUAN   SEOUL   SINGAPORE
SYDNEY   TORONTO

The *McGraw·Hill* Companies

1 2 3 4 5 6 7 8 9 0   DOC/DOC   1 8 7 6 5 4 3 2

ISBN 978-0-07-180995-5
MHID   0-07-180995-3

e-ISBN 978-0-07-180996-2
e-MHID   0-07-180996-1

This publication is designed to provide accurate and authoritative information in regard to the subject matter covered. It is sold with the understanding that neither the author nor the publisher is engaged in rendering legal, accounting, or other professional service. If legal advice or other expert assistance is required, the services of a competent professional person should be sought.

>—*From a Declaration of Principles jointly adopted by
a Committee of the American Bar Association and a
Committee of Publishers*

McGraw-Hill books are available at special quantity discounts to use as premiums and sales promotions, or for use in corporate training programs. To contact a representative please e-mail us at bulksales@mcgraw-hill.com.

This book is printed on acid-free paper.

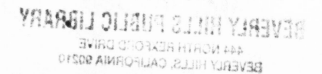

This book is dedicated to four of the most important people in my life, my grandchildren—Jonathan, Sophie, and Gracie Rosen, and Ruby Jane Morris

Contents

Introduction: Why I Wrote This Book

Each of my 12 books is about what I call the "science of investing," the evidence demonstrating the prudent investment strategy. My Only Guides You'll Ever Need series deals with stocks, bonds, alternative investments, and the designing of the right financial plan. My Wise Investing series is a collection of stories and analogies designed to demonstrate that the winning investment strategy is a simple, elegant, and logical one. And because it is so simple, requiring little effort (though lots of discipline), it is also the winning strategy in life.

What I have learned from my experiences is that not many people will devote a lot of time to learn about investing despite its importance. It is difficult to get them to read a 300-page book that cites dozens of studies. That is why I have written this book.

Think, Act, and Invest Like Warren Buffett is designed to explain how adopting some basic principles can help you outperform the vast majority of investors and increase the chances of achieving your financial and life goals.

Over the years, I have talked to thousands of people about investing. I have learned there are some individuals who can be successful investors on their own. If you believe you fall into that category, Chapter 8 provides five important questions for you to answer before you decide to go it alone.

Many others have found great benefit in working with an advisory firm. For those who want to consider working with an advisor, Chapter 8 also provides information on how to perform thorough due diligence as you search for a fiduciary advisor who can truly add value, such as making sure your investment plan is part of an overall financial plan that addresses estate, tax, and insurance issues.

Think, Act, and
Invest Like
Warren Buffett

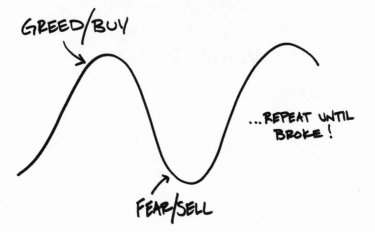

1

Want to Invest More Like Warren Buffett? Start Taking His Advice

f investors were asked, "Who do you think is the greatest investor of our generation?," an overwhelming majority would answer, "Warren Buffett." If they were then asked, "Should you follow the advice of the person you consider the greatest investor?," you would think that they would say, "Yes!" The sad truth is that, while Buffett is widely admired, the majority of investors not only fail to consider his advice but also tend to do *exactly the opposite* of what he recommends.

To demonstrate the truth of this statement, we will review Buffett's investment guidance and see if people have actually followed it. We will review his advice on three issues:

1. Whether you should invest in actively managed or passively managed mutual funds (such as index funds).

2. Whether you should listen to market forecasts.

3. Whether you should try to time the market.

Actively managed funds attempt to uncover and exploit securities the market has "mispriced," buying those they believe are undervalued and avoiding those they believe are overvalued. Actively managed funds may also attempt to time investment decisions to be more heavily invested when the market is rising and less so when the market is falling. In contrast, passively managed funds are basically buy-and-hold vehicles that eschew stock picking and market timing, believing the costs outweigh the benefits. Active investors also look to "experts" for an investing edge, while passive investors ignore such advice.

Before reviewing Buffett's advice, it is important to note that he knows that you cannot invest exactly like he does. You cannot buy entire companies and incorporate them into Berkshire Hathaway, nor can you negotiate special deals during crises, when companies such as Goldman Sachs are willing to pay "top dollar" to have Warren Buffett invest. However, you can follow his guidance about the right investment strategy. As you read Buffett's advice, ask yourself if you have been practicing what he preaches.

Let's begin with Buffett's advice on which type of funds you should invest in.

ACTIVE VERSUS PASSIVE INVESTING

The following are some of the Oracle of Omaha's words of advice on this important decision:

- "By periodically investing in an index fund, the know-nothing investor can actually outperform most investment professionals."[1]

- "Most investors, both institutional and individual, will find that the best way to own common stocks is through an index fund that charges minimal fees. Those following this path are *sure to beat* [emphasis mine] the net results (after fees and expenses) delivered by the great majority of investment professionals. Seriously, costs matter."[2]

- "Over the 35 years, American business has delivered terrific results. It should therefore have been easy for investors to earn juicy returns: all they had to do was piggyback Corporate America in a diversified, low-expense way. An index fund that they never touched would have done the job. Instead many investors have had experiences ranging from mediocre to disastrous."[3]

- "So many investors, brokers and money managers hate to admit it, but the best place for the average retail investor to put his or her money is in index funds."[4]

What is difficult for many investors to understand is that indexing works because *not making* investment decisions (trying to pick stocks or mutual funds or trying to time the market) produces better results than making them. Of course, no one on Wall Street would ever admit that. Remember, Wall Street benefits from the higher fees and greater commissions generated by active strategies. It needs you to play the game of active management because that is its winning strategy.

We now turn to Buffett's advice on whether you should pay attention to economic and market forecasts.

THE VALUE OF FORECASTS

The following is Buffett's advice on whether you should be paying attention to the latest forecasts from so-called economic and market experts:

- "We have long felt that the only value of stock forecasters is to make fortune-tellers look good. Even now, Charlie [Munger] and I continue to believe that short-term market forecasts are poison and should be kept locked up in a safe place, away from children and also from grown-ups who behave in the market like children."[5]

- "A prediction about the direction of the stock market tells you nothing about where stocks are headed, but a whole lot about the person doing the predicting."[6]

Most investors find it hard to believe that their life would be better *without* so much information and that ignoring the investment noise would improve their performance. This leads to the condition I call "CNBC-itis," the need to "tune in." While investors believe they are tuning into valuable information, what they are generally hearing is nothing more than what Jane Bryant Quinn calls "investment porn," and what she feels are "shameless stories about performance that tickle our prurient financial interest."[7] Instead of tuning in, you should be tuning *out*.

Buffett implores investors to ignore forecasts because they tell you nothing about where the market is headed. Research also proves this. The following is a brief summary of that research:

- Economists' forecasting skill has been about as good as guessing. Even those who directly or indirectly run the economy—such as the Federal Reserve, the Council of Economic Advisors and the Congressional Budget Office—have forecasting records worse than pure chance. Even worse, just when you need the forecasts to be most accurate, they have been the most wrong. Economists have not predicted the turning points.[8]

- There have been no economic forecasters who consistently lead the pack in forecasting accuracy.[9]

- Increased sophistication in forecasting has not improved the accuracy of forecasts.[10]

- The only thing that relates to forecasting accuracy has been fame, and the relationship has been negative. The more famous the forecaster, the more inaccurate the forecasts.[11]

Why do investors pay attention to forecasts, ignoring the evidence and Buffett's sage advice? My experience has convinced me that this irrational behavior is caused by an all-too-human need to believe that there is someone who can protect us from bad things, such as bear markets. Unfortunately, there is only one "person" who knows where the market is going. If we ask Him, we won't get an answer, at least not in this lifetime. And in the next one, it won't matter. This is why whenever I am asked about my forecast for the economy or the market, my answer is always the same: "My crystal ball is always cloudy."

What we have learned is that we are no closer to being able to predict the market despite all the innovations in information technology and decades of academic research. The next time you are tempted to act on some guru's latest forecast, ask yourself the following questions:

- Is Warren Buffett acting on this expert's opinion?

- If he isn't, should I be doing so?

- What do I know about the value of this forecast that Buffett (and the market in general) doesn't?

Author Carl Richards, in his book *The Behavior Gap*, recommends asking three questions before you act on someone's advice or forecast:[12]

- If I make this change and I am right, what impact will it have on my life?

- What impact will it have if I am wrong?

- Have I been wrong before?

MARKET TIMING

The following are some of Buffett's admonitions to those who are tempted to time the market:

- "Our favorite holding period is forever."[13]

- "Our stay-put behavior reflects our view that the stock market serves as a relocation center at which money is moved from the active to the patient."[14]

- "Success in investing doesn't correlate with IQ. Once you have ordinary intelligence, what you need is the temperament to control the urges that get other people in trouble investing."[15]

- "Inactivity strikes us as intelligent behavior."[16]

It can be hard to hear that the best course of action during tough market times is to stay the course. Keeping your head while everyone else around you is losing theirs is difficult. It can be even harder to hear that message repeated while things go from bad to worse. However, the message to stay the course is worth repeating because it is the best advice. Because there is no evidence that there are good forecasters, efforts to time the market are highly unlikely to prove productive.

The great irony is that while investors idolize Buffett, they just do not listen to his advice. While investors were pulling hundreds of billions out of the stock market in the wake of the financial crisis of 2008, Buffett was buying. And while investors were once again reacting to the European crisis of 2011, withdrawing almost $100 billion from stock funds over the six months ending October 2011, Berkshire Hathaway was investing almost $24 billion in stocks. It was its largest commitment of new cash in at least 15 years.[17]

Buffett knows that a down market is when investors should be buying, not selling. While he admonishes investors against market timing, he does advise that if you are going to try to time the market, you should buy when everyone else is fearful and sell when everyone else is greedy. What Buffett advises is not to sell (as most individuals do) when expected returns are the greatest (because valuations are low). That is when Buffett is generally a buyer. He is not a buyer because he believes he has a clear crystal ball. Instead, he is buying because expected returns are high: "Whether we're talking about socks or stocks, I like buying quality merchandise when it is marked down."[18] Conversely, the time to be a seller is not when valuations are low and expected returns are high. Buffett offers this advice on the subject:

> The most common cause of low prices is pessimism—sometimes pervasive, sometimes

specific to a company or industry. We want to do business in such an environment, not because we like pessimism but because we like the prices it produces. It is optimism that is the enemy of the rational buyer.[19]

The time to be a seller is when the "coast is clear" and risks appear to be low. That is when valuations are high and expected returns are low. Buying low and selling high is a much better strategy than the reverse, which is what most investors do.

The appealing thing is that there is a simple strategy that allows you to invest more like Warren Buffett, buying when valuations are low and expected returns are high, and selling when valuations are high and expected returns are low. All you need is the discipline to ignore your emotions and adhere to your investment plan, which should require regular rebalancing. Rebalancing, or the process of restoring a portfolio to its original composition, is integral to the winning investment strategy. It requires you to buy what has done relatively poorly (at relatively low valuations) and sell what has done relatively well (at relatively high valuations). However, it is not easy to maintain the discipline to stay the course because "CNBC-itis," and the emotions it causes, often get in the way.

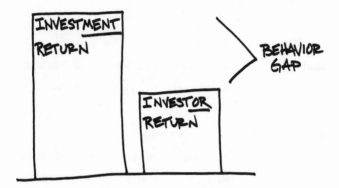

2

Want to Invest More Like Warren Buffett? Start Thinking Like He Does

In order for you to learn to invest like Warren Buffett, you have to learn how to think like him. That is what this chapter is all about. It provides you with three important insights that will help you become Buffett-like in your approach to investing. First, you'll learn the right way to think about bad news. Next, you'll learn how to avoid the mistake most investors make of engaging in what is referred to as "stage-one" thinking. Instead, you will learn to think ahead, engaging in "stage-two" thinking. And finally, you'll learn not only how important it is to have a well-developed plan but also how critical it is to adhere to it.

UNDERSTAND HOW TO THINK ABOUT BAD NEWS

One of the secrets to Buffett's success as an investor is that during bear markets he is able to keep his head while everyone else around him is losing theirs. He understands that bad news doesn't mean stock prices have to go lower. The market price already reflects all publicly available information. That means that markets can be expected to continue to fall only if future news is worse than already expected. If the news is no worse than expected, you will earn high returns resulting from the low valuations. And even if the future news is not good but is better than expected, valuations will rise as the risk premium demanded by the market begins to fall. That's often how bull markets begin.

It is totally irrelevant to stock prices whether news is good or bad. Failing to understand this basic tenet causes investors to react to the news and get overenthusiastic when news is good and panic when news is bad. In order to be a successful investor, what you need to understand is whether the news is better or worse than *already expected*. In other words, what matters is not whether news is good or bad but whether or not it is a surprise. Let's take a look at an example.

The year 2010 was miserable for the commercial real estate industry, as mortgage defaults multiplied. In 2008, just 1 percent of commercial loans were delinquent. In 2009, the default rate jumped to 6 percent. In 2010, the rate jumped to 9 percent. Given that horrible news, one would expect that investors in commercial mortgages would have suffered greatly. Despite the dramatic increase in defaults, 2010 was a great year for investors in commercial mortgages as prices soared. For example, junior AAA-rated bonds went from 30 cents on the dollar to almost par (or 100 cents on the dollar).[1]

The contrast between the rising default rate and the rising value of commercial mortgages seems at first to be contradictory. The explanation is that prices rose because the default rates, while bad, were not nearly as bad as the market expected. As a result, market prices rose, reflecting the prevailing view that default losses would not be so great as to damage the upper (more highly rated) tranches of the securitization ladder.

The bottom line is this: if you want to invest more like Buffett, you must understand that surprises are a major determinant of stock performance. Because they are unpredictable and instantly incorporated into prices, you are best served by ignoring the news, because acting on it is likely to prove counterproductive.

AVOID STAGE-ONE THINKING

One of the keys to Buffett's success as an investor is that he avoids the tendency to engage in what Thomas Sowell called "stage-one" thinking, a weakness of most investors. They see the crisis and the risks but cannot see beyond that. Their stomachs take over, they cannot control their emotions, panic sets in, and well-developed plans are abandoned.

Buffett engages in "stage-two" thinking. He expects that a crisis will lead governments and central bankers to come up with solutions to address the problem. And the greater the crisis, the greater the response is likely to be. That allows him to see beyond the crisis, enabling his head to keep control over his stomach and his emotions. The next time you find yourself reacting to a crisis, ask yourself:

- Am I engaging in stage-one thinking?

- Do I know something the market doesn't?

- Is the news already incorporated into prices?

- Do I want to sell when valuations are low and expected returns are high?

- Will governments and central banks do nothing? Or will they address the problem?

- Have I reacted in the past to such events? How did that turn out?

Most important, you need to ask this question: If I sell now, how will I know when it is safe to buy again? This is the big problem for those who sell during crises.

Is There Ever a Green Flag?

There is another problem for those who are tempted by the latest crisis to sell and wait for safer times. If you go to the beach to ride the waves and you want to know if it is safe, you simply look to the lifeguard stand. If the flag is green, it is safe. If it is red, it is too dangerous to take a chance. For many investors, the market often looks too dangerous. So they do not want to buy, or they decide to sell.

Here is the problem. While the surfer can wait a day or two for the ocean to calm down, there is never a green flag saying it is safe to invest. The markets faced a litany of problems from March 9, 2009, through March 30, 2011. There was never a green light. It was red the entire time. That is why investors were pulling out hundreds of billions of dollars from the market, missing the greatest rally since the 1930s, with the S&P 500 providing a return of more than 100 percent. So if you decide to sell, you are virtually doomed to fail while you wait for the next green flag.

Even worse is what happened to some investors who thought they saw a green flag. Consider this sad tale of an investor who watched the S&P 500 fall from about 1,450 in February 2007 all the way to 752 on November 20, 2008. Worn out by the wave of bad news, he sold. However, he knew there was a problem. With interest rates at their then current levels, he could not achieve his financial goals without taking risks. So he designed a strategy to get back in. He would wait until next year to see if the market recovered. By January 6, 2009, the S&P 500 had risen almost 25 percent to 935. Of course, he had missed that rally while he waited for that green flag. But now he felt that it was once again safe to buy. Unfortunately, by March 9, 2009, the S&P 500 had dropped back all the way to 677. So he sold again, and the market began its fierce rally. In my opinion, he'll have a very difficult time reaching his investing goals. The problem is that once you sell you are virtually doomed to fail. The green flag you are waiting for will never appear. Never. Buying when valuations are high and selling when they are low explains why so many investors have taken all the risks of stocks but have earned bond-like returns.

Understanding the fallibility of individual investors is why Buffett offered these words of wisdom:

- "The most important quality for an investor is temperament, not intellect."[2]

- "Investing is simple, but not easy."[3]

While it is simple to invest more like Buffett—you just need a well-designed plan and have the discipline to stick to it—it is not easy. Emotions, such as fear and panic in bear markets and greed and envy in bull markets, cause even well-developed plans to end up in the trash heap. The stomach takes over from the head . . . and stomachs do not make good decisions.

If you want to invest more like Buffett, you are going to have to learn to control your emotions. The best way of preventing your stomach from taking over is to stop paying attention to forecasters and so-called experts.

HAVE A PLAN AND STICK TO IT

Warren Buffett's other passion is bridge. He once said: "I wouldn't mind going to jail if I had three cellmates who played bridge." Noting the similarity between bridge and investing, he stated: "The approach and strategies are very similar." He added: "In the stock market you do not base your decisions on what the market is doing, but on what you think is rational."[4] With bridge, you need to adhere to a disciplined bidding system. While there is no one best system, there is one that works best for you. Once you choose a system, you need to stick with it.

Similarly, with investing, in order to be successful you must have a "system," a plan that determines your asset allocation based on your unique ability, willingness, and need to take risk. Just as there is no one best bidding system, there is no one *best* asset allocation. However, there is one that is *right* for you. Once you develop your plan, and put it in writing, you need to stick to it. Here is Buffett's advice on the subject: "Once you have ordinary intelligence, what you need is the temperament to control the urges that get other people into trouble in investing."[5]

INVESTORS WORSHIP BUT IGNORE THE ORACLE OF OMAHA

Having completed our review of Buffett's advice, it is time now to answer the following questions:

1. Do you act on market forecasts?

2. Do you try to time the market?

3. Have you sold after markets have experienced big losses, only to then buy again after they have recovered?

4. Have you adhered to an investment policy statement and your asset allocation, only rebalancing and tax managing as required?

If, in answering the questions above, you recognize that you have been engaging in destructive behavior, then you have taken the first step on the road to recovery. However, because crises are the norm, you will continue to be tested. Just as there are no ex-alcoholics, just recovering ones, there are no ex-market timers, just recovering ones. That explains why while there are tens of millions of investors who idolize the Oracle of Omaha, there are few individual investors who actually act in the market like Warren Buffett. However, you can be one of the few if you make up your mind to do it.

Buffett knows that the winning investment strategy is really simple. However, he also acknowledges that it is not easy, because emotions get in the way of being able to maintain discipline and adhere to a well-developed plan.

The remainder of this book is designed to help you play the winner's game, providing the simple prescriptions for success. The rest is up to you.

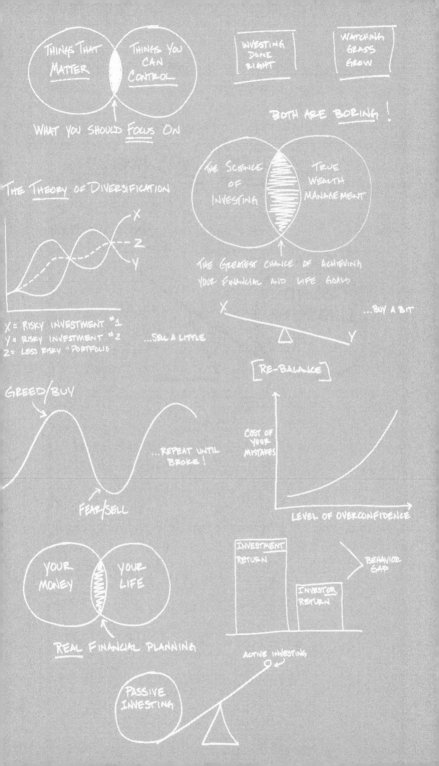

WEIGHT OF EVIDENCE

~ 3 ~

Should You Be an Active or a Passive Investor?

There are two competing theories about investing. The conventional wisdom is that markets are inefficient; they persistently misprice assets. If that is true, smart, hardworking people can uncover which stocks the market has under- or overvalued and make money by loading up on undervalued ones or avoiding (or even shorting) overvalued ones. They can think, "Intel is trading at 20, and we should load up on it because it is really worth 30," or, "We should avoid it because it is really worth 10." This is called the art of stock selection. And if markets misprice assets, smart people can also time the market—raising their stock allocations and getting in ahead of the bull emerging into the arena and lowering their stock allocations before the bear emerges from its hibernation. This is called the art of market timing. Together, they make up the art of active management.

The competing theory is that *markets are efficient.* Hence, the price of a security is the best estimate of the correct price. If markets are efficient, attempts to outperform them are highly unlikely to prove productive, especially after expenses. *This does not mean it is impossible to beat the market. Given the tens of thousands of professionals (and millions of individuals) engaging in the effort, we should expect some to randomly succeed even over long periods of time.*

In order to have the best chance of achieving your financial goals, you need to decide which theory and strategy is the most prudent. The problem is how to know whether an active or a passive strategy is the wisest. Despite the fact that money may be the third most important thing in our lives (not money itself, but what money provides) after our family and our health, our education system has totally failed to equip investors with the knowledge to determine the answer to our question. Unless you have an MBA in finance, it is likely that you have never taken even a single course in capital markets theory.

Additionally, you are likely to get a biased answer from either Wall Street or the financial media. Wall Street wants and needs you to play the game of active investing so they make money by charging high fees for active management and through commissions and bid-offer spreads whenever you trade. The financial media also wants and needs you to "tune in."

THE EVIDENCE

Fortunately, there is a large body of evidence on the inability of active management to deliver *alpha*: performance above appropriate risk-adjusted benchmarks (such as comparing the performance of a small-cap fund to a small-cap index, not to the S&P 500 Index). As the Carl Richards sketch shows, the weight of evidence is heavily in favor of passive investing. The following are short summaries of the volumes of academic research on the efforts of individual investors, mutual funds, and pension plans to generate alpha. Remember, if markets are inefficient, we should see evidence of the persistent ability to outperform appropriate risk-adjusted benchmarks. And that persistence should be greater than randomly expected.

Individual Investors

We begin with exploring the evidence on the performance of individual investors. It clearly demonstrates that individuals are playing a loser's game, enriching only the purveyors of products and services. The following is a summary of the evidence:

- The stocks that both men and women bought subsequently underperformed, and the stocks they sold outperformed after they were sold.[1]

- Both men and women underperformed market and risk-adjusted benchmarks.[2]

- Those who traded the most performed the worst.[3]

- The more confident people were in their ability to either identify mispriced securities or time the market, the worse the results.[4]

- Men produced similar gross returns to women. However, men earned lower net returns as their greater turnover negatively impacted results.[5]

- Single women produced better net returns than their married counterparts, presumably because they were not influenced by their over-confident spouses.[6]

- Demonstrating that more heads are not better than one, the average investment club lagged a broad market index by almost 4 percent per year. Adjusting for risk, the performance was even worse. And clubs would have been better off never trading during the year.[7]

- Demonstrating that intelligence did not translate into higher returns, the Mensa (the high IQ society) investment club underperformed the S&P 500 Index by almost 13 percent per year for 15 years.[8]

Exacerbating the problem is that investors are unaware of how poorly they are doing. A study on the subject found investors overestimated their own performance by an astounding 11.5 percent a year. And the lower the returns, the worse investors were when judging their realized returns. While just 5 percent believed they had experienced negative returns, the reality was that 25 percent did so, and more than 75 percent underperformed the relevant benchmark.[9]

Actively Managed Mutual Funds

The following is a brief summary of the evidence on the inability of actively managed funds to deliver out-performance:

- There has been no evidence of the ability to persistently generate outperformance beyond what would be randomly expected. The past performance of active managers is not pro-logue.[10]

- Expenses reduced returns on a one-for-one basis (each dollar spent reduced returns by approximately the same amount) and explained much of the persistent long-term underperformance of mutual funds.[11]

- Turnover reduced pretax returns by almost 1 percent of the value of the trade.[12]

- In its own study, Morningstar found that expense ratios were a better predictor than its star ratings. Simply ranking by expenses produced superior results—the lowest cost funds tended to produce the highest returns.[13]

The bottom line is that the costs of security selection and market timing prove a difficult hurdle
to overcome. And despite what most people believe,
even long periods (such as 10 or even 15 years) of superior performance do not have predictive value; we
cannot differentiate between skill and luck. One reason for this is that successful active management contains the seeds of its own destruction: the hurdles to
generating alpha increase as the amount of assets under management increase. This is an important con-
tributor to the lack of persistent performance, even in
the presence of skill.[14]

This body of evidence is likely what led Buffett to
draw this conclusion:

> By periodically investing in an index fund the
> know–nothing investor can actually outperform
> most investment professionals.[15]

Pension Plans

It seems logical to believe that if anyone could beat
the market, it would be the pension plans of U.S. companies. Why is this a good assumption? Let's consider:

- Pension plans control large sums of money, giving them access to the best and brightest portfolio managers.

- Plans do not hire managers with a record of underperformance.

- Most pension plans hire professional consultants to help them perform due diligence in interviewing, screening, and ultimately selecting the very best managers. These consultants employ armies of talented people who, you can be certain, have thought of every conceivable screen.

- Their fees are much lower than the fees individual investors pay.

- Because pension plans are exempt from taxation, they do not have the burden of taxes to pay that individuals must overcome.

Here's the evidence on the performance of pension plans:

- Plan sponsors hired investment managers who had outperformed. However, the outperformance didn't continue, as the post-hiring excess returns were indistinguishable from zero. If plan sponsors had stayed with the fired investment managers, their returns would have been greater than those actually delivered by the newly hired managers.

- There was no evidence the number of managers beating their benchmarks was greater than pure chance.[16]

Studies on the performance of corporate 401(k) plans have found the same type of evidence: there is no ability to identify *ahead of time* the few active funds that will outperform their appropriate benchmarks.[17] As you can see, the evidence is overwhelming that passive investing is the winner's game. Active management is the loser's game because the odds of winning are so low that it is not prudent to try. In addition to the evidence, Nobel Laureate William Sharpe provided us with a simple and elegant proof of why active management must be, in aggregate, a loser's game.[18]

THE ARITHMETIC OF ACTIVE INVESTING

The market is made up of only two types of investors: active and passive. Assume that 70 percent of investors are active and 30 percent of investors are passive. Also assume the market returns 10 percent. (The outcome is the same regardless of the percentages used.) On a pre-expense basis, passive investors must earn 10 percent. What rate of return, before expenses, must the active managers, in aggregate, have earned? Because the sum of the parts must equal the whole, collectively, active managers must also have earned 10 percent. The following equations show the math:

Total Market	=	Active Investors	+	Passive Investors
(10%)	=	(70% x ?)	+	(30% x 10%)
(10%)	=	(70% x 10%)	+	(30% x 10%)

It does not matter what percentages of market share you use; the outcome is the same. The reason is that all stocks must be owned by someone. If one active investor outperforms because he overweighted the top-performing stocks, another active investor must have underperformed by underweighting those very same stocks. In aggregate, on a pre-expense basis, active investors earn the same market rate of return as do passive investors. This holds true no matter what asset class or type of market.

THE MATH IS ALWAYS THE SAME

If, instead of using the total stock market, we substituted any other index or asset class, we would come to the same conclusion. That exposes the myth that active management works in "inefficient" asset classes like small-cap and emerging market stocks.

The same thing is true for bull and bear markets. If the market loses 10 percent, the Vanguard Total Stock Market Fund will also lose 10 percent on a pre-expense basis. In aggregate, so must active investors. The math does not change for bull or bear markets.

So far, we have been discussing gross (before expenses) returns. Unfortunately, you do not earn gross returns; you earn returns net of expenses. To get to the net returns, the only kind you get to spend, we must subtract all costs:

- Expenses: the operating expenses of the fund

- Trading costs: the fund's costs of buying or selling securities

- Bid-offer spreads: the difference between the asking price (the price you pay when you buy) and the bid price (the price you receive when you sell)

- Brokerage commissions

- Market impact: the additional costs incurred while transacting large blocks of stock, resulting from changes in price before the full amount is bought or sold

- Cost of cash: the difference between the returns earned while sitting in cash and what would have been earned if fully invested

Because active funds have higher expenses in each category, the cost of implementing a passive strategy will be less than that of an active one. Thus, in aggregate, passive investors must earn higher net returns than active investors. The mathematical facts cannot be denied. Active management is, in aggregate, a negative sum (loser's) game.

The evidence is overwhelming that the surest way to win the game of active management is to refuse to play. Thus, the winning strategy is to adopt a passive investment strategy. You can do that by investing in index mutual funds, such as those of Vanguard, Charles Schwab, and Fidelity. You can also consider investing in exchange-traded funds (ETFs)—such as iShares and SPDRs—which are essentially mutual funds that trade on exchanges throughout the day like stocks.

Another option are the passively managed funds (which, though passive, are not index funds) offered by fund families such as Bridgeway, Dimensional Fund Advisors, Invesco (through its PowerShares funds), and WisdomTree. Well-designed, passively managed funds can add value over similar index funds by maximizing the benefits of indexing (such as low cost, broad diversification, low turnover, and tax efficiency) while minimizing some of the negatives (such as forced turnover, which increases trading costs and creates tax inefficiencies).

Now that you know the right strategy, let's turn our attention to the development of a financial plan.

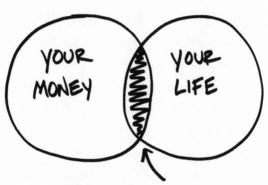

REAL FINANCIAL PLANNING

4

The Need to Plan: It Is Not Only About Investments

ould you take a trip to a place you have never been without a road map, directions, or a GPS? Would you start a business without spending lots of time and energy thoroughly researching that business and then writing a well-designed plan? The answers explain why the old and wise saying holds true: those who fail to plan, plan to fail.

Despite the wisdom of this statement, the vast majority of investors begin their investment journey without a plan, specifically, an investment policy statement (IPS) laying out the plan's objectives and the road map to achieving them. One reason so few investors have a well-developed, written, and signed plan (what you should consider a contract between you and yourself) is that Wall Street and the media do not really want you to have one. The winning strategy for them is the losing strategy for you.

It is important to understand that a plan is necessary in order to make rational decisions about investments. You cannot properly evaluate any investment without considering how its addition affects the risk and expected return of your portfolio, and thus the odds of achieving the plan's objectives.

A Financial Plan Must Be a Living Document

Just as a business plan must be reviewed regularly to adapt to changing market conditions, an IPS and a financial plan must be living documents. If any of your plan's underlying assumptions change, the IPS should be altered to adapt to the change. Life-altering events (such as a birth or death in the family, a marriage or divorce, a large inheritance, or a promotion or job loss) can affect the plan in dramatic ways. Thus, the IPS should be reviewed whenever a major life event occurs.

Market movements can also lead to changes in your assumptions. Bull markets may mean you're ahead of your goals, allowing you to take less risk. But, bull markets also lower expected future returns, meaning those still far from their goals may have to take more risk. (This does not mean you should take more risk. An alternative is to lower the goal.) The reverse is true of bear markets. A good policy is to review the IPS and its assumptions on an annual basis.

Before writing an IPS, you should thoroughly review your financial and personal status. You should consider not only your personal financial situation but also such factors as

- The stability of your job

- Whether the risk of your job is highly correlated with your stocks holdings

- Your investment horizon

- Your tolerance for risk

- The need for emergency reserves

Keep in mind that your investment horizon extends well beyond your planned retirement date. And it may even extend beyond your death if you are investing on behalf of your heirs.

You should also consider your need to take risk. Have you already saved enough? If so, why continue taking risk? Far too many investors fail to understand that the strategy to get rich (take risks) is entirely different from the strategy to stay rich (minimize risks, diversify the risks you take, and don't spend too much).

It is also important to understand that it's not enough to have only a well-developed investment plan. It needs to be incorporated into an overall financial plan that also addresses estate and tax planning issues, as well as risk management issues such as the need for life, health, disability, long-term care, personal liability, and longevity insurance. It should also incorporate a plan for when to begin taking social security. Finally, your charitable intentions should be addressed.

A well-developed plan should also address such issues as objectives for transferring wealth and your values to family members. This can be incorporated into what is called a *family wealth mission statement.* You should consider having your children (and their spouses, if any) involved in your estate plan, including reading your will and understanding your intentions with respect to your property upon your death. They should also know the family's net worth. And they should get to know your advisors (your attorney, accountant, and financial advisor).

It is also important to develop a contingency plan in case your portfolio fails to deliver the returns that your plan anticipated. You should put in writing what actions you will take if a bear market leads to there being an unacceptable chance of your plan failing. You do not want to find yourself in a situation where your portfolio is likely to run out of assets or jeopardize an important legacy goal.

Your plan should list the specific actions. These actions might include delaying retirement or returning to the workforce, reducing current spending, reducing the financial goal, selling a home, or moving to a location with a lower cost of living.

The written IPS should include a list of your specific goals, such as the amount you plan to add to your portfolio each year, the amount of assets you are trying to accumulate by a certain date, when you plan to begin withdrawals from the portfolio, and the dollar amount you plan on withdrawing each year. This will allow you to track progress toward the goal, making appropriate adjustments along the way.

The next step in developing your IPS is to specify your asset allocation, or the makeup of your portfolio.

The IPS should include a formal asset allocation table identifying both the target allocation for each asset class and the rebalancing targets in the form of minimum and maximum tolerance boundaries. A written IPS serves as a guidepost and helps provide the discipline needed to adhere to a strategy over time. Developing that asset allocation plan is the subject of the next chapter.

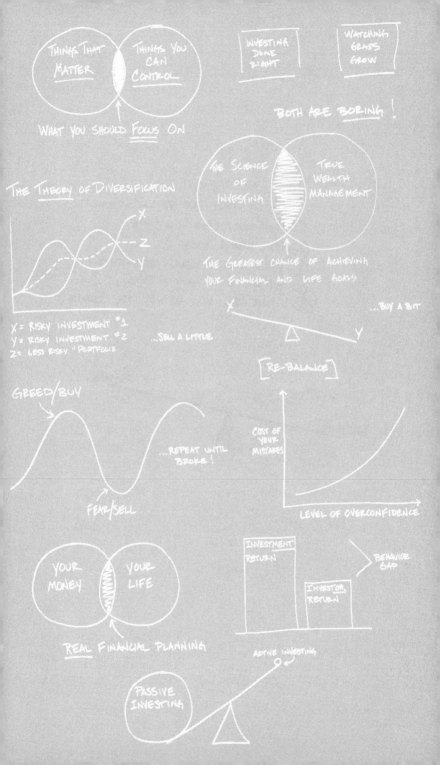

THE 5 BIG QUESTIONS:
① HOW MUCH CAN YOU SAVE?
② HOW MUCH RISK?
③ HOW MUCH WILL YOU NEED?
④ WHEN WILL YOU NEED IT?
⑤ WHAT DO YOU WANT TO LEAVE?

5

How Much Risk Should You Take? The Asset Allocation Decision

There's no one plan that's right for everybody. The amount of risk you should take and the makeup of your portfolio depends entirely on your unique ability and willingness and need to take risk. Let's begin with taking a look at the ability to take risk.

THE ABILITY TO TAKE RISK

The longer your investment horizon, the more risk you can take. This is because you have a greater ability to wait out a bear market. In addition, the longer the investment horizon, the more likely stocks will provide higher returns than bonds. The following table can help serve as a guideline to help you determine how to divide your assets between riskier stocks and safer bonds.

Investment Horizon	Maximum Stock Allocation (%)
0–3 Years	0
4 Years	10
5 Years	20
6 Years	30
7 Years	40
8 Years	50
9 Years	60
10 Years	70
11–14 Years	80
15–19 Years	90
20 Years or longer	100

Besides your investment horizon, you should also consider your labor capital. We can define labor capital as the present value of future income derived from labor. It is an asset that does not appear on any balance sheet. It is also an asset that is not tradable like a stock or a bond. Thus, it is often ignored, at potentially great risk to the individual's financial goals. There are several important points to consider about your labor capital.

First, when we are young, human capital is at its highest point. It is also often the largest asset individuals have when they are young. As we age and accumulate financial assets, and the time we have remaining in the labor force decreases, the amount of human capital relative to financial assets shrinks. This shift over time should be considered in terms of the asset allocation decision.

Second, we need to consider not only the magnitude of our human capital but also its volatility. Some people (such as tenured professors and government employees) have stable jobs. Their labor income is much like a bond. Other people (such as commissioned salesmen and construction workers) have labor income that is more volatile and, thus, acts more like stocks. Your asset allocation should incorporate these important points.

Third, you should consider the significance of human capital as a percentage of total assets. If human capital is a small percentage of the total portfolio (because there are large financial assets), the volatility of the human capital and its correlation to financial assets becomes less of an issue.

Fourth, to avoid having too many eggs in one basket, you should avoid investing in assets that have a high correlation with your human capital. Unfortunately, far too many people follow Peter Lynch's advice to "buy what you know." The result is that they invest heavily in the stocks of their employers. This is a mistake on two fronts. The first is that it is a highly undiversified investment. The second is that the investment is likely to have a high correlation with the person's human capital. Employees of such companies as Enron and WorldCom found out how costly a mistake that can be.

Fifth, human capital can be lost because of two risks that need to be addressed by means other than through investments. The first is the possibility of disability. This risk can be addressed by the purchase of disability insurance. The other risk is that of mortality. That issue can be addressed with the purchase of life insurance. These issues highlight the importance of integrating your investment plan into an overall estate, tax, and risk management plan.

There is one more important issue we need to consider about the ability to take risk: the need for liquidity. The need for liquidity is determined by the need for near-term cash requirements as well as the potential for unanticipated calls on capital. A good rule of thumb is to have a reserve to cover six months of ordinary expenses.

THE WILLINGNESS TO TAKE RISK

The willingness to take risk is determined by what could be called the "stomach acid" test. Ask yourself this question: Can you stick with your investment strategy when markets crash? Successful investment management depends on your ability to withstand periods of stress and overcome the severe emotional hurdles present during bear markets like the ones experienced in 1973–1974, 2000–2002, and 2008. Thus, it is important not to take more risk than your stomach can handle. And besides, life is too short not to enjoy it.

The following table provides a guideline for you to consider. The maximum tolerable loss is independent of the time frame.

Maximum Tolerable Loss (%)	Maximum Stock Exposure (%)
5	20
10	30
15	40
20	50
25	60
30	70
35	80
40	90
50	100

THE NEED TO TAKE RISK

The need to take risk is determined by the rate of return required to achieve your financial objectives. The greater the rate of return needed, the more risk you need to take. However, you should also make sure you distinguish between real needs and desires. These are very personal decisions, with no right answers. However, the fewer things that fall into the needs column, the lower the need to take risk. Conversely, the more things that fall into the needs column, the more risk one will have to take.

THE MAKEUP OF
THE PORTFOLIO

Once we have addressed the key issues of ability, willingness, and need to take risk, we need to decide on the makeup of the portfolio. Volumes of research have found that the vast majority of the risk and expected return of your portfolio are determined by its asset allocation, meaning the percent of your portfolio devoted to specific asset classes. More specifically, it's determined by the exposure to what are called risk factors. Riskier assets have higher *expected* (not guaranteed) returns. If the higher returns were guaranteed, there would be no risk. We begin our discussion with the broad category of stocks.

Stocks

In order of importance, the first decision is to determine how much of an allocation you will have to riskier stocks versus bonds. Since stocks are riskier than bonds, they provide greater *expected* returns.

The next decision involves dividing up your stock allocation among U.S. stocks, international stocks (the stocks of other developed countries), and emerging-market stocks. Within those three stock categories, you can divide your allocations further into small-cap or large-cap and value or growth.

Similar to the way stocks have higher expected returns than bonds because they are riskier, small-cap and value stocks have higher expected returns than their large-cap and growth counterparts. However, those higher expected returns come with additional risk. In other words, the higher expected returns of small-cap and value stocks are not a free lunch; they are compensation for accepting incremental risk.

In addition to providing higher expected returns, small-cap and value stocks provide another benefit: they help to diversify your portfolio. The reason for this is that some of the risks of small-cap stocks and of value stocks are unique. We can see that when we look at correlations of returns—the degree to which the historical returns of these asset classes have a tendency to vary together. From 1927 through 2011, the correlation of the small-cap premium to the equity premium has been only about 0.4. The correlation of the value premium to the equity premium has only been about 0.1. And there has been virtually no correlation of the small-cap premium to the value premium. The low correlations show that the small-cap premium and the value premium are *independent* (unique) risk factors. That makes them good diversifiers of the risks of stocks in general. We can see the benefit of diversification by examining the returns of three asset classes for the years 1998 and 2001.

In 1998, while the S&P 500 Index rose almost 29 percent, small-cap stocks (as represented by the CRSP 6-10 Index) lost about 2 percent and small-cap value stocks (as represented by the Fama-French Small Value Index ex utilities) lost 10 percent. The relative performances reversed in 2001. While the S&P 500 Index lost 12 percent, small-cap stocks gained almost 18 percent and small-cap value stocks gained over 40 percent.

Now consider a portfolio that owned an equal amount of each asset class. In 1998, it would have earned about 5 percent. In 2001, it would have earned about 15 percent. Diversifying across all three asset classes would have provided a much smoother ride than if you had invested all your eggs in any of the three baskets. Since no one has demonstrated the ability to determine ahead of time which asset class *will do well when*, the winning strategy is to diversify your risks. Similar examples could be shown for international and emerging market stocks. The bottom line is that since diversification is the only free lunch in investing, you might as well eat a lot of it.

Bonds

Bonds have two risk factors: term (number of years to maturity) and default (credit). The longer the term to maturity and the lower the credit rating, the greater the risk and *expected* returns. So you need to decide how much you will allocate to high-quality versus lower-quality bonds, and how much you will allocate to short-term and intermediate-term bonds versus long-term bonds.

Before you tackle the type of bonds to own, it is critical that you understand the role bonds should play in a portfolio. The central role of bonds in a portfolio should be to dampen the risk of the overall portfolio to an acceptable level, which means you should minimize risks in your bond holdings. That makes the investment decision simple. A basic rule of thumb is to limit your holdings to FDIC-insured CDs and the safest bonds, those that carry the full faith and credit of the U.S. government, and highly rated (AAA/AA) municipal bonds. If you choose to own corporate bonds (which entail more credit risk), the historical evidence suggests that you limit your holdings to those with remaining maturities of three years or less and to bonds that have investment-grade ratings (a rating that indicates that the bond has a relatively low risk of default). These guidelines simplify your decision.

Alternative Investments

The search for better performing investments typically leads investors to consider what are often called *alternative investments.* This term is generally used to describe investments beyond the familiar categories of stocks and investment-grade bonds. The category includes such investments as real estate, commodities (e.g., precious metals, oil and gas, and wheat), private equity, venture capital, hedge funds, junk bonds, emerging market bonds, convertible bonds, preferred stocks, and so-called structured investment products. A common element of alternative investments is that Wall Street typically makes a lot of money as the purveyors of these products. The good news is that, with the exception of real estate and commodities, the academic research demonstrates that you should not even consider owning any of the other alternatives. You certainly do not need them to develop a well-diversified portfolio or to achieve your goals.

The two alternatives worth considering are real estate and commodities. Real estate is a good diversifier of the risks of both stocks and bonds. And you can invest in real estate by owning an index fund (such as Vanguard's REIT Index Fund) that invests in a broad spectrum of publicly traded real estate investment trusts (REITs). Similarly, commodities are a good diversifier of the risks of stocks and bonds. And there are good mutual fund and ETF alternatives for investing in commodity indexes (the best way to access this asset class).

We now turn our attention to the asset location decision, or the best places to hold your various investments to gain a tax advantage. What should be your preference for holding your various investments in your taxable (individual, community property, trust, etc.) and tax-advantaged accounts, such as IRA, 401(k), or 403(b) plans?

THE ASSET
LOCATION DECISION

When faced with a choice of placing assets in either taxable or tax-advantaged accounts, taxable investors should have a preference for holding stocks (versus bonds) in taxable accounts. *However, before investing any taxable dollars, investors should always first fund their Roth IRA or deductible retirement accounts.* And because tax-advantaged accounts are the most tax-efficient investment accounts, *you should always take complete advantage of your ability to fund them.* The one exception is the need to provide liquidity for unanticipated funding requirements.

If you invest in either REITs or commodities, because they are tax-inefficient investments, the preference should ordinarily be to hold these investments in tax-advantaged accounts. If you cannot do so, you should consider passing on their diversification benefits.

Once you decide on your asset allocation you will need to also decide on whether you should invest in mutual funds or individual securities.

MUTUAL FUNDS OR INDIVIDUAL SECURITIES?

When implementing your plan, you will have to decide between investing in individual securities and using mutual funds and ETFs. To make the right choice, you need to be able to distinguish between two very different types of risk: good risk and bad risk. Good risk is the type you are compensated for taking. For example, you cannot diversify away the risks of investing in stocks no matter how many you own. The compensation you receive for taking the risks comes in the form of greater *expected* returns.

On the other hand, bad risk is the type for which there is no such compensation. Thus, it is called *uncompensated* or *unsystematic* risk. One example of bad or uncompensated risk is the risk of the individual company (such as Enron or Lehman Brothers). The risks of individual stock ownership can be easily diversified away by owning index funds that basically own all the stocks in an entire asset class/index. These vehicles eliminate the single-company risk in a low-cost and tax-efficient manner.

You can also diversify asset class risk by building a globally diversified portfolio, allocating funds across various asset classes: domestic, international, and emerging markets; large-cap and small-cap; value and growth; and real estate and commodities.

Because these risks can be diversified, the market does not compensate investors for taking such risks. The same is true of staying within a single asset class. This is why investing in individual companies and only one or a few asset classes has more in common with speculating than it does with investing. Investing means taking compensated risk. Speculating is taking uncompensated risk. Other examples of uncompensated risk are investing in sector funds (such as health care or technology) and individual country funds (other than a U.S. total stock market fund).

Prudent investors recognize the difference between speculating and investing. They take only risks for which they are compensated. Thus, when it comes to investing in risky assets, the only vehicles you should consider are mutual funds. This advice applies to all risky assets, not just stocks, but corporate bonds as well.

With bonds backed by the full faith and credit of the U.S. government, the lack of credit risk means you can buy individual bonds and save the expense of a mutual fund. On the other hand, mutual funds, in addition to providing the benefits of diversification, also provide the benefit of convenience, including the automatic reinvestment of interest. That benefit is at least worth considering.

We now turn to demonstrating the benefits of building a globally diversified portfolio.

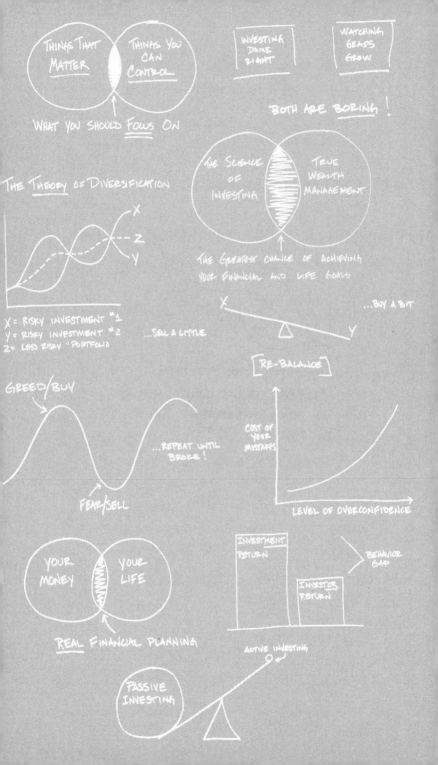

THINGS THAT MATTER

THINGS YOU CAN CONTROL

WHAT YOU SHOULD FOCUS ON

INVESTING DONE RIGHT

WATCHING GRASS GROW

BOTH ARE BORING!

THE SCIENCE OF INVESTING

TRUE WEALTH MANAGEMENT

THE GREATEST CHANCE OF ACHIEVING YOUR FINANCIAL AND LIFE GOALS

THE THEORY OF DIVERSIFICATION

X
Z
Y

X = RISKY INVESTMENT #1
Y = RISKY INVESTMENT #2
Z = LESS RISKY "PORTFOLIO"

...SELL A LITTLE

...BUY A BIT

X
Y

RE-BALANCE

GREED/BUY

...REPEAT UNTIL BROKE!

FEAR/SELL

COST OF YOUR MISTAKES

LEVEL OF OVERCONFIDENCE

YOUR MONEY

YOUR LIFE

REAL FINANCIAL PLANNING

INVESTMENT RETURN

INVESTOR RETURN

BEHAVIOR GAP

ACTIVE INVESTING

PASSIVE INVESTING

THE THEORY OF DIVERSIFICATION

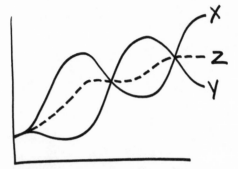

X = RISKY INVESTMENT #1
Y = RISKY INVESTMENT #2
Z = LESS RISKY "PORTFOLIO

6

How to Build a Well-Designed Portfolio

As discussed in Chapter 5, diversification is the only free lunch in investing. Unfortunately, most investors fail to take advantage of this "all-you-can-eat" opportunity because they do not build well-diversified portfolios. Instead, they hold a portfolio that consists of just a handful of stocks. They do so because they make mistakes, such as being over-confident in their investment skills. They also tend to confuse the familiar with the safe, causing them to concentrate their holdings in companies they are familiar with, particularly the stock of their employer. This tendency typically results in minimal exposure to international stocks.

Because most investors have not studied financial economics or read financial economic journals, or books on modern portfolio theory, they do not have an understanding of how many stocks are needed to build a truly diversified portfolio. To effectively diversify the risks of just the asset class of U.S. large-cap stocks, you would have to hold a minimum of 50 stocks. For U.S. small-cap stocks the figure is much higher. Once you expand your investment universe to include international stocks, it becomes obvious that the only way to effectively diversify a portfolio is through the use of mutual funds.

However, even when individuals invest in mutual funds, they typically do not diversify effectively because they make the mistake of thinking that diversification is about the number of funds they own. Instead, it is about how well one's investments are spread across different asset classes. For example, an investor who owns 10 different actively managed U.S. large-cap funds may believe that he is effectively diversified. While it is true that each fund will likely have some differentiation in its holdings from the others, collectively, all the investor has done has been to create an expensive "closet" index fund. The reason for this is that it is likely that the return of his portfolio, before expenses, will approximate the return of an S&P 500 Index fund. After expenses, the odds are great it will underperform.

Even many individuals who invest in index funds get it wrong because they limit themselves to funds that mimic either the S&P 500 Index or a total U.S. market index. At the very least, they should also include a significant allocation (30 to 50 percent) to an international fund, such as Vanguard's Total International Stock Index Fund.

MODERN PORTFOLIO THEORY AT WORK

The next step is to show you how simple it is to build a more effective, globally diversified portfolio. Many investors think that diversification means owning enough mutual funds. However, the key is spreading them across asset classes. After all, 10 different large-cap growth funds still mean you only have exposure to one asset class.

We will begin with a portfolio that has a conventional asset allocation of 60 percent stocks and 40 percent bonds. The time frame will be the 37-year period,

1975–2011. This period was chosen because it is the longest for which we have data on the indexes we need. While maintaining the same 60 percent stock/40 percent bond allocation, we will then expand our investment universe to include other stock asset classes.

Step 1: We create a portfolio that consists of just two investments: the S&P 500 Index for the stock allocation and five-year Treasury notes (the highest-quality intermediate-term bond) for the bond portion. We will see how the portfolio performed if one had the patience to stay with this allocation from 1975 through 2011 and rebalanced annually. We will then demonstrate how the portfolio's performance could have been made more efficient by increasing its diversification across asset classes. We do so in four simple steps.

> *Portfolios are shown for illustrative purposes only. Indexes are not available for direct investment. Their performance does not reflect the expenses associated with the management of an actual portfolio, nor do indexes represent results of actual trading.*

Portfolio 1

| S&P 500 Index | 60% |
| Five-Year Treasury Notes | 40% |

1975–2011

Annualized Return (%)	Annual Standard Deviation (%)
10.6	10.8

By changing the composition of the control portfolio, we will see how we can improve the efficiency of our portfolio. To avoid being accused of data mining, we will alter our allocations by arbitrarily "cutting things in half."

Step 2: We begin by diversifying our stock holdings to include an allocation to U.S. small-cap stocks. Therefore, we reduce our allocation to the S&P 500 Index from 60 to 30 percent and allocate 30 percent to the Fama/French Small Cap Index. (The Fama-French indexes measure returns using the academic definitions of asset classes. Note that utilities have been excluded from the data.)

Portfolio 2

S&P 500 Index	30%
Fama/French Small Cap Index	30%
Five-Year Treasury Notes	40%

1975–2011

	Annualized Return (%)	Annual Standard Deviation (%)
Portfolio 1	10.6	10.8
Portfolio 2	11.7	11.4

Step 3: Next, we diversify our domestic stock holdings to include value stocks. We shift half of our 30 percent allocation in the S&P 500 Index to a large-cap value index and half of our 30 percent allocation of small-cap stocks to a small-cap value index.

Portfolio 3

S&P 500 Index	15%
Fama/French US Large Value Index (ex utilities)	15%
Fama/French US Small Cap Index	15%
Fama/French US Small Value Index (ex utilities)	15%
Five-Year Treasury Notes	40%

1975–2011

	Annualized Return (%)	Annual Standard Deviation (%)
Portfolio 1	10.6	10.8
Portfolio 2	11.7	11.4
Portfolio 3	12.2	12.5

Step 4: Our next step is to shift half of our stock allocation to international stocks. For exposure to international value and international small-cap stocks we will add a 15 percent allocation to both the MSCI EAFE Value Index and the Dimensional International Small Cap Index.

Portfolio 4

S&P 500 Index	7.5%
Fama/French US Large Value Index (ex utilities)	7.5%
Fama/French US Small Cap Index	7.5%
Fama/French US Small Value Index (ex utilities)	7.5%
MSCI EAFE Value Index	15%
Dimensional International Small Cap Index	15%
Five-Year Treasury Notes	40%

1975–2011

	Annualized Return (%)	Annual Standard Deviation (%)
Portfolio 1	10.6	10.8
Portfolio 2	11.7	11.4
Portfolio 3	12.2	12.5
Portfolio 4	12.4	11.8

Step 5: The effect of the changes has been to increase the return on the portfolio from 10.6 percent to 12.4 percent—an increase of 17 percent in relative terms. This outcome is what we should have expected to see as we added riskier small-cap and value stocks to our portfolio. Thus, we also need to consider how the risk of the portfolio was impacted by the changes. The standard deviation (a measure of volatility, or risk) of the portfolio increased from 10.8 percent to 11.8 percent—an increase of 8 percent in relative terms. While returns increased 17 percent, volatility increased just 8 percent.

There is one more asset class we want to consider including in a portfolio. As we discussed earlier, commodities diversify some of the risks of investing in stocks. They also diversify the risks of investing in bonds. Therefore, we will add a 4 percent allocation to the Goldman Sachs Commodity Index, reducing each of our 4 domestic stock allocations by 0.5 percent and both the international stock allocations by 1 percent.

Portfolio 5

S&P 500 Index	7%
Fama/French US Large Value Index (ex utilities)	7%
Fama/French US Small Cap Index	7%

Fama/French US Small Value Index (ex utilities)	7%
Dimensional International Small Cap Index	14%
MSCI EAFE Value Index	14%
Goldman Sachs Commodity Index	4%
Five-Year Treasury Notes	40%

1975–2011

	Annualized Return (%)	Annual Standard Deviation (%)
Portfolio 1	10.6	10.8
Portfolio 2	11.7	11.4
Portfolio 3	12.2	12.5
Portfolio 4	12.4	11.8
Portfolio 5	12.1	11.2

Most investors think of commodities as risky investments. However, you will note that the addition of commodities to the portfolio actually reduced the volatility of the portfolio, and reduced it by twice the reduction in the portfolio's return. Whereas the portfolio's return fell by 0.3 percent, its standard deviation fell by 0.6 percent. Relatively speaking, the portfolio's return fell 2 percent while its volatility fell by 5 percent. This "diversification benefit" is why you should consider including a small allocation to commodities in your portfolio.

The net result of all of our changes is that we increased the return of the portfolio by 1.5 percent, from 10.6 to 12.1 percent—an increase of 15 percent in relative terms. At the same time, the volatility of the portfolio increased just 0.4 percent, a relative increase of 4 percent.

LOWERING THE PORTFOLIO RISK

You have now seen the power of modern portfolio theory at work. You saw how you can add risky (and, therefore, higher expected returning) assets to a portfolio and increase the returns more than the risks were increased. That is the benefit of diversification. However, there is another way to consider using this knowledge. Instead of trying to increase returns without proportionally increasing risk, we can try to achieve the same return while lowering the risk of the portfolio. To try and achieve this goal, we increase the bond allocation to 60 percent from 40 percent and decrease the allocations to each of the stock asset classes and to commodities.

Portfolio 6

S&P 500 Index	4.5%
Fama/French US Large Value Index (ex utilities)	4.5%
Fama/French US Small Cap Index	4.5%
Fama/French US Small Value Index (ex utilities)	4.5%
Dimensional International Small Cap Index	9.5%
MSCI EAFE Value Index	9.5%
Goldman Sachs Commodity Index	3%
Five-Year Treasury Notes	60%

1975–2011

	Annualized Return (%)	Annual Standard Deviation (%)
Portfolio 1	10.6	10.8
Portfolio 2	11.7	11.4
Portfolio 3	12.2	12.5
Portfolio 4	12.4	11.8
Portfolio 5	12.1	11.1
Portfolio 6	10.9	7.9

Compared with Portfolio 1, Portfolio 6 achieved a higher return with far less risk. Portfolio 6 provided a 0.3 percent higher return, 10.9 percent versus 10.6 percent—a relative increase of 3 percent. It did so while experiencing 2.9 percent lower volatility,

7.9 percent versus 10.8 percent—a relative decrease of 27 percent.

PLAYING THE WINNER'S GAME

Through the step-by-step process described above, it becomes clear that one of the major criticisms of passive portfolio management—that it produces *average* returns—is wrong. There was nothing "average" about the returns of any of the portfolios. Certainly the returns were greater than those of the average investor with a similar stock allocation, be it individual or institutional.

Passive investing delivers *market*, not average, returns. And it does so in a relatively low-cost and tax-efficient manner. The average actively managed fund produces below-market results, does so with great persistency, and does so in a tax-inefficient manner.

By playing the winner's game of accepting market returns, you will almost certainly outperform the vast majority of both individual and institutional investors who choose to play the active game. There is only one caveat. You must learn to think of yourself akin to a postage stamp. The lowly postage stamp does only one thing, but it does it exceedingly well: it sticks to its letter until it reaches its destination. *You must stick to your investment plan until you achieve your financial goals.* Your only activities should be rebalancing, managing for taxes, and adjusting the plan if the underlying assumptions change. And that is the subject of our next chapter.

X

...BUY A BIT

...SELL A LITTLE

Y

[RE-BALANCE]

～ 7 ～

The Care and Maintenance of Your Portfolio

Just as a garden must undergo regular care and maintenance, regular maintenance must be performed on an investment portfolio. Otherwise, you will lose control over the most important determinant of risk and returns: your portfolio's asset allocation. That makes rebalancing one of the two important items on the portfolio maintenance agenda. The other is tax management. We will discuss both, beginning with rebalancing.

REBALANCING

Rebalancing restores the portfolio to your desired risk profile, the one you wrote in your IPS. Without regularly rebalancing a portfolio, you will find that "style drift" will occur. In rising markets, your portfolio will become more aggressive as your stock holdings become a bigger percentage of your portfolio. Without rebalancing, your stock allocation will typically be increasing when valuations are higher and, thus, expected returns are lower. In falling markets, the reverse is true. Your stock allocation will typically be decreasing when valuations are lower and, thus, expected returns are higher. That does not sound like an intelligent approach.

Buy Low and Sell High

The rebalancing process is simple, though not easy. This is because emotions can get in the way. Rebalancing allows you to reduce your allocation in the asset classes that performed relatively the best (selling high) and increase the position in the asset classes that performed relatively poorly (buying low). Isn't it every investor's dream to buy low and sell high?

Another benefit of rebalancing is that over time it will produce a bonus—the portfolio's annualized return will exceed the *weighted average* of the annualized returns of the component asset classes. This is referred to as a *diversification return,* or "rebalancing bonus." And the more volatile the asset classes are within the portfolio, and the lower their correlations, the greater the effect of rebalancing. The reason is that when you rebalance you will be buying at lower lows and selling at higher highs.

An important decision to make is how to determine the rebalancing parameters. The following will provide you with a reasonable rule of thumb to consider.

The 5/25 Percent Rule

Rebalancing may cause transaction fees to be incurred, and it may also have tax implications. Therefore, it should be done only whenever new funds are available for investment or when your asset allocation has shifted substantially out of alignment. A reasonable rule of thumb is to use a 5/25 percent rule in an asset class's allocation before rebalancing. That is, rebalancing should occur only if the change in an asset class's allocation is greater than either an absolute 5 or 25 percent of the original target allocation, whichever is less.

For example, let's assume an asset class was given an allocation of 10 percent of the portfolio. Applying the 5 percent rule, one would not rebalance unless that asset class's allocation had either risen to 15 percent or fallen to 5 percent. However, using the 25 percent rule, one would reallocate if it had risen or fallen by just 2.5 percent to either 12.5 or 7.5 percent.

In this case, the 25 percent figure was the governing factor. If one had a 50 percent asset-class allocation, the 5/25 percent rule would cause the 5 percent figure to be the governing factor since 5 percent is less than 25 percent of 50 percent, which is 12.5 percent. In other words, one rebalances if either the 5 percent or the 25 percent test indicates the need to do so.

While rebalancing should be done based on risk (as described above), not on the calendar, if you are doing it yourself, keep it simple and apply the 5/25 percent test at least quarterly. You should be sure that the test is applied at all three levels:

- The broad level of stocks and bonds

- The level of domestic and international asset classes

- The more narrowly defined individual asset-class level (such as emerging markets, real estate, small-cap, value, and so on).

For example, suppose you had six stock asset classes, each with an allocation of 10 percent, resulting in a stock allocation of 60 percent. If each stock class appreciated so that it then constituted 11 percent of the portfolio, no rebalancing would be required if you only looked at the individual asset-class level (the 5/25 percent rule was not triggered). However, looking at the broader stock class level, we see that rebalancing is required. With six stock asset classes, each constituting 11 percent of the portfolio, the stock asset class as a whole is now at 66 percent. The increase from 60 to 66 percent triggers the 5/25 percent rule. The reverse situation may occur where the broad asset classes remain within guidelines but the individual classes do not. Once again, just as with the model portfolios, the 5/25 percent test is just a guideline. You can create your own guideline for rebalancing for risk. The discipline the process provides is more important than the percentages you choose.

The IPS Asset Allocation and Rebalancing Table

Your IPS should include an asset allocation and rebalancing table. The table should include both the target levels for each asset class and the minimum and maximum levels to which the allocations will be allowed to drift. Some drift should be allowed to occur, because rebalancing generally involves costs, including transaction fees and taxes in taxable accounts.

Sample Rebalancing Table Using 5/25 Rule

Asset Class	Minimum Allocation (%)	Target Allocation (%)	Maximum Allocation (%)
U.S. large	7.5	10	12.5
U.S. large value	7.5	10	12.5
U.S. small	7.5	10	12.5
U.S. small value	7.5	10	12.5
Real estate	7.5	10	12.5
Total U.S.	**45**	**50**	**55**

Asset Class	Minimum Allocation (%)	Target Allocation (%)	Maximum Allocation (%)
International large value	3.75	5	6.25
International small	3.75	5	6.25
International small value	3.75	5	6.25
Emerging markets	3.75	5	6.25
Total International	**15**	**20**	**25**
Total Stock	**65**	**70**	**75**
Nominal Bonds	7.5	10	12.5
TIPS	15	20	25
Total Bonds	**25**	**30**	**35**

The Rebalancing Process

In the accumulation phase, there are two ways to rebalance. The first is to sell what has done relatively well in order to buy what has done relatively poorly. The second is to use new cash to raise the allocations of the asset classes that are below targeted levels. A combination of the two strategies can be used. Utilizing new cash is preferred; it reduces transactions costs, and it reduces or eliminates the capital gains that are generated when selling appreciated assets in taxable accounts. In the withdrawal phase, investors can sell what has done relatively well.

A strategy to consider is to have distributions paid in cash, rather than automatically reinvested, and use the cash to rebalance. However, you should consider the size of the portfolio and any transaction costs that might be incurred. For small accounts where transaction costs are present, this might not be a good strategy. Here are some other recommendations on the rebalancing process:

* Consider if incremental funds will become available in the near future (such as a tax refund, a performance bonus, proceeds from a sale, or dividends). If capital gains taxes will be generated by rebalancing, it might be prudent to wait until the new cash is available.

* Consider delaying rebalancing if it generates significant short-term capital gains. The size of the gain should be a major consideration: the larger the gain, the greater is the benefit of waiting to receive the more favorable treatment that long-term gains receive. Also consider

how long it will be before additional funds can be generated to rebalance.

- If significant capital gains taxes are generated, consider rebalancing to only the minimum/maximum tolerance ranges rather than restoring allocations to the target levels.

We now turn to the other important maintenance item: tax management.

TAX MANAGEMENT

While the winning strategy is to use a passive investment strategy, passively managing the taxable portion of the portfolio without regard to taxes is a mistake. An investor can improve the after-tax returns of a portfolio by proactive tax management. Tax management involves the following actions:

- Choose the most tax-efficient vehicles.

- Sell funds with losses throughout the year—whenever the value of the tax deduction significantly exceeds the transaction costs—and immediately reinvest the proceeds in a manner that avoids the wash-sale rule (which would cause the tax deduction to be disallowed). A *wash sale* occurs when you sell securities at a loss and then buy or contract to buy substantially identical securities within 30 days. Portfolios should be checked regularly (at least quarterly) to determine if there are opportunities to harvest losses. Waiting until the end of the year to perform tax-loss harvesting is a mistake, because losses that might exist early in the year may no longer exist by the end of the year.

- Sell the highest cost-basis lots first to minimize gains and maximize losses. As of 2012, custodians are required to track this information for you.

- In general, never willingly realize short-term gains. Instead, wait until the gains qualify as long term. Note that if your stock allocation is well above target, you may wish to override this suggestion, weighing the risks of an "excessive" allocation to stocks versus the potential tax savings. Another common exception is if you have prior capital gains losses that can offset these gains.

- Trade around dividend dates. Shares of a fund should not be purchased just prior to the date of record for dividend payments to shareholders. Note that the ex-dividend date is not the same as the date of record. The date of record is the date when you must be on the company's books as a shareholder to receive the dividend. The ex-dividend date is the date after the record date when the dividend is "separated" (the payment is made) from the fund. The fund then trades at a lower price, net of dividends. Depending on the size of the distribution that is expected, you should not consider buying within 30 to 60 days of the ex-dividend date.

- Trade around year-end distributions. Most funds make distributions once a year, usually in December. Some funds make them more frequently, and sometimes they make special distributions. Check to see if there are going to be large distributions that will be treated as either ordinary income or short-term gains. If you are considering buying a fund around the time of the distribution, it may make sense to wait until after such a distribution has been paid out, thereby avoiding having to pay tax on the taxable portion of those gains on your income tax return. If you are considering selling a fund, you might benefit from selling the fund before the record date. By doing so, the increase in the net asset value will be treated as long-term capital gains, and taxes will be at the lower long-term rate. If the fund making the large payout is selling for less than your tax basis, consider selling the fund prior to the distribution. Otherwise, you will have to pay taxes on the distribution, despite having an unrealized loss on the fund. Also, consider the potential distribution from any replacement fund so you don't exacerbate the problem.

We next turn to the question of whether you should be a do-it-yourself investor or hire an advisor.

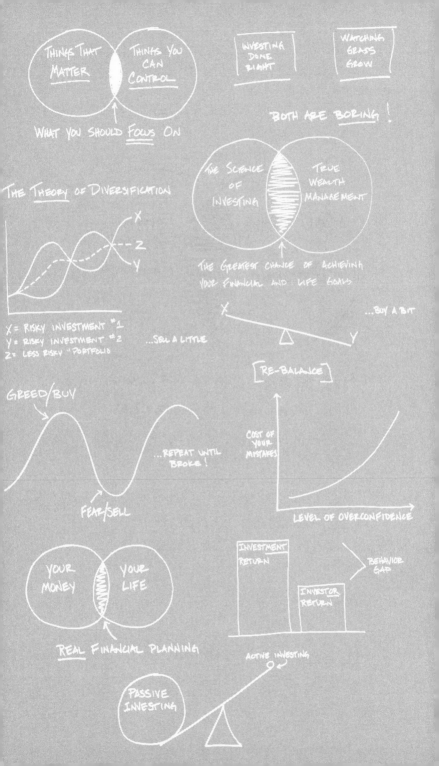

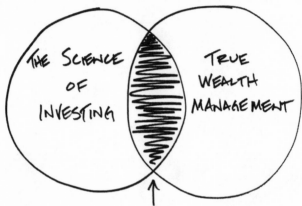

THE GREATEST CHANCE OF ACHIEVING YOUR FINANCIAL AND LIFE GOALS

~ 8 ~

Should You Hire a Financial Advisor?

Whether we are talking about home repairs or investing, individuals can be categorized into two broad groups: those who hire professionals and the "do-it-yourselfers"—those who do not want to pay professionals for something they believe they can do just as well. Of course, some who belong to the do-it-yourself group would be better off hiring professionals. One reason is that if something is not done right the first time, the cost of correcting errors can far exceed the cost of a professional to do it right in the first place. Another is that while you can recover from making a mistake while trying to fix a leaky faucet, the damage done by financial errors can take years to recover from and can even be irreversible.

If you are considering being a do-it-yourself investor, ask yourself the following five questions:

1. Do I have all the knowledge needed to develop an investment plan, integrate it into an overall estate, tax, and risk management (insurance of all types) plan, and then provide the ongoing care and maintenance that is required?

2. Do I have the mathematical skills needed? It helps to have knowledge that goes well beyond simple arithmetic, including advanced knowledge of probability theory and statistics, such as correlations and the various moments of distribution (such as skewness and kurtosis).

3. Do I have the ability to determine the appropriate asset allocation, one that provides the greatest odds of achieving my financial goals while not taking more risk than I have the ability and willingness to take? An important part of the planning process includes the use of a Monte Carlo simulator (a sophisticated retirement planning program) to estimate the odds

of achieving your financial goals under various asset allocations, saving, and spending assumptions. Required assumptions include expected returns of asset classes, expected standard deviations of asset classes, and expected correlations among asset classes. There are many of these programs available, several of which have serious flaws. And because of their complexity, it is easy to make mistakes.

4. Do I have a strong knowledge of financial history? One needs to be aware of how often stocks have provided negative returns, how long bear markets have lasted, and how deep they have been. Those who do not know their history are likely to repeat past mistakes.

5. Do I have the temperament and the emotional discipline needed to adhere to a plan in the face of the many crises I will almost certainly face? Are you confident that you have the fortitude to withstand a severe drop in the value of your portfolio without panicking? Will you be able to rebalance back to your target allocations (keeping your head while most others are losing theirs), buying more stocks when

the light at the end of the tunnel seems to be a truck coming the other way? Think back to how you felt and acted after the events of September 11, 2001, and during the financial crisis that began in 2007. Experience demonstrates that fear often leads to paralysis, or, even worse, panicked selling and the abandonment of well-developed plans. When subjected to the pain of a bear market, even knowledgeable investors who know what to do fail to do the right thing because they allow emotions to take over, overriding what their brains know is the correct action to take. This results in what Carl Richards calls "the behavior gap." The term is used to describe the failure of investors to earn the same return as that earned by the very funds in which they invest. Ask yourself: Have I always done the right thing? Have my returns matched those of my investments?

If you have passed this test, you are part of a small minority. This book provides you with not only the winning strategy of broad global diversification and passive investing but also guidance on how to construct a portfolio to address your unique circumstances. And the book's conclusion contains my list of the 30 Rules of Prudent Investing that will help you achieve your goals. If you are interested in learning more about how to develop an overall financial plan that is tailored to your unique situation, read *The Only Guide You'll Ever Need for the Right Financial Plan.*

Alternatively, you may recognize that you do not have the knowledge, temperament, or discipline to succeed on your own. And even if you decide that you meet these requirements, you may recognize that a good financial advisory firm can add value in many ways, including freeing you to focus your attention on the most important things in your life, such as time spent with family, friends, or meaningful endeavors. Thus, you may place a greater value on that time than the cost spent on advice. It is a choice about finding the right balance in your life.

If you decide to hire a financial advisory firm, that choice will be one of the most important decisions you will ever make, because it will have the greatest impact. Thus, it is critical that you get it right. Here is valuable advice: there are three criteria that should be absolutes when searching for the right advisor. These criteria are

- A fiduciary standard of care

- Advice based on science (evidence from peer-reviewed journals), not opinions

- Investment planning that has been integrated into an overall financial plan

A FIDUCIARY STANDARD OF CARE

There are two standards of care that financial professionals operate under: fiduciary and suitability. Under a fiduciary standard, the finance professional must always act in your best interests. Under a suitability standard, the finance professional only has to buy products that are suitable. They don't necessarily have to be in your best interest. There is no reason why you should settle for anything less than a fiduciary standard. And there is no reason you should ever work with an advisor or firm not prepared to meet this standard. The bottom line is this: you must be convinced that the guiding principle of the advisor or firm is that advice offered is solely in your best interest.

There are several things you can do in your due diligence to give you the best chance to receive unbiased advice. First, require that the advisory firm serve as a fee-only advisor, which avoids the conflicts that commission-based compensation can create. With commission-based compensation, it can be difficult to know if the investment or product recommended by the advisor is the one that is best for you or the one that generates greater compensation for the advisor. Avoiding commissioned-based compensation helps to ensure that the advice you receive is client-centric; the only thing being "sold" is advice and solutions to problems, not products.

Second, you need to make sure that all potential conflicts of interest are fully disclosed. Along with asking questions, you should review the firm's Form ADV—a disclosure document setting forth information about the firm's advisors, its investment strategy, fee schedules, conflicts of interest, regulatory incidents, and more. Careful due diligence helps minimize the risk of an expensive mistake.

Third, you should require that the firm's advisors invest their personal assets (including the firm's profit-sharing and/or retirement plan) based on the same set of investment principles and in the same or comparable securities that they recommend to their clients. Although you should expect to see asset allocations different from those that are being recommended to you (as each investor has his, own unique circumstances), the investment vehicles should be the same.

EVIDENCE-BASED ADVICE

You should consider working only with a firm whose investment strategy and advice is based on the science of investing, not on opinions. To demonstrate the wisdom of this advice, consider the following situation. You are not feeling well. You make an appointment to visit a doctor your friend has recommended. The doctor's job is to diagnose the problem and recommend treatment. After a thorough exam, he turns around to his bookshelf and reaches for the latest copy of *Prevention* magazine. Before hearing his advice you are probably already thinking it is time to get a second opinion. Therefore, you make an appointment with another doctor. After her exam, she reaches for a copy of the *New England Journal of Medicine*. At this point, you are feeling much better about the advice you are about to receive. The financial equivalents of the *New England Journal of Medicine* are such publications as the *Journal of Finance*. The advisory firm should be able to cite evidence from peer-reviewed journals supporting their recommendations. You should not be getting your advice from the finance equivalents of *Prevention,* such as *Investor's Business Daily* or *Barron's.*

INTEGRATED FINANCIAL PLANNING

Because plans can fail for reasons that have nothing to do with an investment plan, it is critical that the advisory firm you choose will integrate an investment plan into an overall estate, tax, and risk management plan.

A well-developed financial plan includes a detailed analysis of the need for

- Life insurance, for replacing income, paying estate taxes and/or transferring wealth to heirs or a charity

- Disability insurance, in case you can't work

- Longevity insurance, to cover the risk of running out of money because you live longer than expected, a risk that can be hedged through the purchase of a payout annuity

- Long-term care insurance, to protect against care costs draining your assets

- Property and casualty insurance, such as for homes, cars, and boats and against floods and earthquakes

- Personal liability insurance, including an umbrella (excess liability) policy

It is important to understand that plans can fail even when estate planning is done well. For example, far too often individuals pay for high-powered attorneys to develop well-thought-out estate plans only to have the trusts created either go totally unfunded or be funded with the wrong type of assets. Some trusts are designed to generate stable cash flows and should be funded with safe bonds. Others are designed with a growth objective in mind and should be funded primarily with stocks.

Estate plans can also derail you because the beneficiaries have not been properly named (resulting from a failure to update documents to address life events such as divorce or death) or because the type or method of asset distribution is inappropriate (for instance, directing assets to be distributed directly to a beneficiary with demonstrated creditor, bankruptcy, or financial management issues). This is another example of why a financial plan must be a living document, one that is reviewed on a regular basis.

It is also critical to understand that estate plans can fail despite the best efforts of top-notch professional advisors. Unfortunately, it is not uncommon for estates to lose their assets and for family harmony to splinter following the transition of the estate. This occurs because beneficiaries are unprepared, they do not trust one another, and communications break down. While great attention is typically paid to preparing the *assets* for transition to the beneficiaries, very little, if any, attention is being paid to preparing the *beneficiaries* for the assets they will inherit. A good advisory firm can add great value by helping to prepare and educate beneficiaries for the wealth they will inherit.

There are many other ways a good financial advisory firm can and should add value. The following is a partial list:

- Retirement planning, including cash withdrawal strategies. Choosing the most efficient amount and account from which assets should be withdrawn as well as the sequencing can

make a big difference in after-tax results. Another critically important decision is when to
begin taking social security.

- Regular, ongoing communications, especially
  during times of crisis. Education protects you
  from having your emotions take control of
  your portfolio.

- Ongoing education about innovations in finance. The knowledge of how markets work ad-
  vances on a persistent basis. Thus, you should
  be sure that the firm has the depth of resources
  to stay on top of the latest research.

- The ability to analyze complex financial products, helping you avoid purchasing costly
  products that are meant to be sold, not bought.

- Disciplined cost- and tax-effective rebalancing
  and tax management that are not driven by the
  calendar but by how the portfolio's assets are
  performing.

- College funding.

- Selecting investments for 529 plans, 401(k),
  403(b), and other employer plans.

- Gifting to heirs and charities in the most effective manner.

- Home purchase and mortgage financing decisions.

- The management and ultimate disposition of large concentrated positions with low-cost basis (typically the stock of your employer or stock that has been inherited).

- Separate account management of bond portfolios, eliminating the expense of a mutual fund, while maximizing tax efficiency and after-tax returns.

- Ongoing performance tracking, measuring the progress versus your plan and recommending adjustments that are necessary to prevent failure.

- Acting as an "insurance policy" in the event of a death of a family member who is responsible for managing financial matters.

Clearly, no one advisor can be an expert in all of these areas. Therefore, when choosing a firm, be sure that it has a team of experts who can help address each of these areas. You should also make sure that the firm's comprehensive wealth management services are provided by individuals who have the PFS (personal financial specialist), CFP (certified financial planner), or other comparable designations. Note that the PFS credential is granted to CPAs who have demonstrated their knowledge and expertise in personal financial planning. And once these designations are granted, they must be maintained through required professional development to keep them current.

It is also important to be clear that the firm will deliver a high level of personal attention and develop strong personal relationships. This should be part of your due diligence process as you check the firm's reputation with other local professionals (such as CPAs and attorneys) and client references.

Another part of your investigation should be asking the advisor how he or she spends time at work. You might ask: "Can you please tell me about your average day?" What you are looking for is an advisor who spends the majority of his or her time solving client's concerns about such issues as

- Making smart decisions about money

- Minimizing income, gift, and estate taxes

- Transferring assets to the next generation

- Protection from third parties unjustifiably taking their assets

- Interest in making significant charitable gifts

Your investigation should include sharing all of your concerns with the advisor. The objective is to develop a deep understanding of how the advisor can help you address these concerns and ensure that you are confident you have a high level of trust in the advisor, his or her support team, and the advisory firm as a whole.

There is one last point we need to cover. As is the case with the choice of investment vehicles, with choice of investment advisors costs matter. But what *really* matters is the value added relative to the cost. The lowest cost investment vehicle may not be the best choice. Remember that while good advice doesn't have to be expensive, bad advice almost always will cost you dearly, no matter how little you pay for it.

The choice of a financial advisor is one of the most important decisions you will ever make. That is why it is so important to perform a thorough due diligence. The bottom line is that you want to be sure that the firm you choose is one where the science of investing meets true wealth management and that the services are delivered in a highly personal manner.

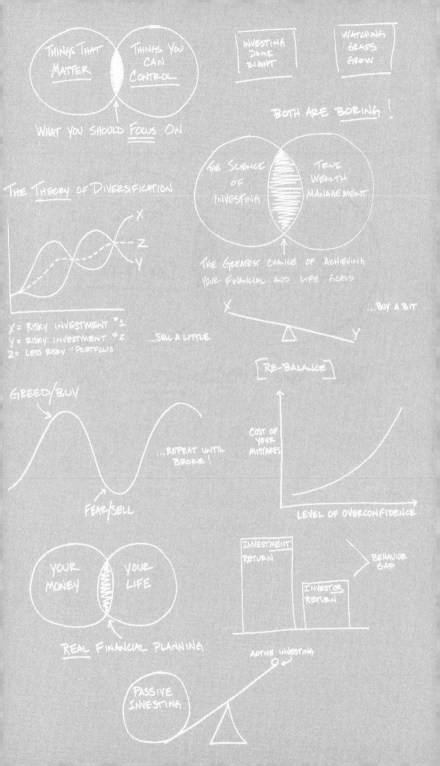

THINGS THAT MATTER — THINGS YOU CAN CONTROL

WHAT YOU SHOULD FOCUS ON

INVESTING DONE RIGHT

WATCHING GRASS GROW

BOTH ARE BORING!

THE THEORY of DIVERSIFICATION

X
Z
Y

THE SCIENCE OF INVESTING — TRUE WEALTH MANAGEMENT

THE GREATEST CHANCE OF ACHIEVING YOUR FINANCIAL AND LIFE GOALS

X = RISKY INVESTMENT #1
Y = RISKY INVESTMENT #2
Z = LESS RISKY "PORTFOLIO

...SELL A LITTLE

X
Y
...BUY A BIT

[RE-BALANCE]

GREED/BUY

...REPEAT UNTIL BROKE!

FEAR/SELL

COST OF YOUR MISTAKES

LEVEL OF OVERCONFIDENCE

YOUR MONEY — YOUR LIFE

REAL FINANCIAL PLANNING

INVESTMENT RETURN

INVESTOR RETURN

BEHAVIOR GAP

PASSIVE INVESTING

ACTIVE INVESTING

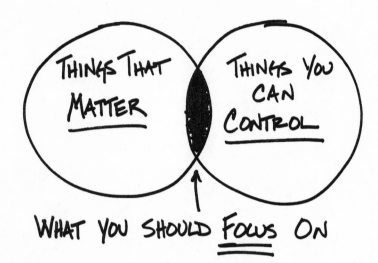

9

Winning the Game of Life

As we discussed in Chapter 3, there is an overwhelming body of evidence demonstrating that passive investing is the prudent investment strategy. Passive investing also allows you to win the far more important game: the game of life. The following tale demonstrates the wisdom of that statement.

An expert in time management was invited to speak to an MBA class. After a brief introduction she reached down and produced a very large mason jar and set it on a table in front of her. She then reached down again and produced a box filled with big rocks. She proceeded to remove the rocks from the box and carefully placed them, one at a time, into the jar. When no more rocks would fit inside the jar, she asked the class, "Is this jar full?" Everyone yelled, "Yes." She then reached under the table, pulled out a bucket of gravel, dumped some in, and shook the jar. This caused pieces of gravel to work themselves down into the spaces between the big rocks. She continued this process until no more gravel could be placed into the jar. She then asked the class, "Is the jar full?" One student, getting the idea, answered, "No." She then reached under the table, brought out a bucket of sand, and started dumping the sand into the jar. The sand began to fill the spaces between the rocks and the gravel. She continued until no more sand could fit into the jar. Once more she asked, "Is this jar full?" This time everyone shouted, "No!" She then grabbed a pitcher of water and poured until the jar was filled to the brim. She then asked the class, "What is the moral of the story?" An eager student raised his hand and said, "The moral of the story is that no matter how full your schedule is, you can always fit in one more meeting!"

The speaker replied, "Nice try, but that is not the moral of the story. The truth this illustration teaches us is that if you do not put the big rocks in first, you can never get them in." To each of us, the "big rocks" mean something different, but at the core, the big rocks are those things that provide the richest meaning to our lives.

As a passive investor, when I come home from my busy day, I get to sit down with a glass of wine and ask my wife about her day and how my kids and grandchildren are doing. Because I did not spend my time trying to beat the market, I also got to coach my youngest daughter's softball, soccer, and basketball teams. I also read about 70 books each year, do community service, play tennis, and focus on the other big rocks, the really important things in my life.

Investors following an active management strategy spend much of their precious leisure time watching the latest business news, studying the latest charts, reading financial trade publications, and so on. What they are really doing is focusing on the gravel, the sand, and the water. Therefore, even if they are among the very few who are successful at the game of active investing, the "price" of success may be that they lose the far more important game of life.

The question for you to consider is, what are the big rocks in your life? Is the big rock in your life trying to generate extra returns through active management strategies that require you to "invest" large amounts of your time? Or are the big rocks in your life time spent with your loved ones, your faith, your education, your dreams, a worthy cause, or teaching or mentoring others? If you do not already know the answer, perhaps this story will help you find it.

Shortly after my first book was published in 1998, I received a call from a doctor. He had been in practice just a few years. He had a wife and a young child, with another child on the way. He had gotten caught up in the euphoria of the bull market and the advent of day trading. He had seen many of his doctor friends generate large profits from trading stocks, and he thought he should get in on this easy money.

After putting in his typical long day he would head straight for his computer and the Internet. He spent hours studying charts and investment reports and following the chat boards. Within a few months he had turned his small investment stake into about $100,000. Unfortunately, his wife no longer had a husband, and his child no longer had a father. He was now married to his investments. His wife began to seriously question their marriage. *Luckily*, within a few months he had lost all his profits.

Fortunately, the doctor realized that his original gains were likely a matter of luck and that he had been a beneficiary of a bull market. More important, he recognized that he was not paying attention to his family. When discussing this with a friend, his friend suggested that he read *The Only Guide to a Winning Investment Strategy You'll Ever Need*. After doing so he called to thank me for helping him find the winner's game in investing, but more to the point, for helping him find the winner's game in life. From then on he knew to focus on the big rocks in his life.

The following is another true story. About one year after my first book was published, I met Rick Hill. Rick was a sophisticated investor with an MBA from Wharton, University of Pennsylvania. Rick had about 30 years of experience in financial management. After meeting with one of my partners, and having read my book, Rick became a client. Eventually, Rick joined Buckingham Asset Management as a financial advisor so that he could help others enjoy the benefits of passive investing. Upon joining, he related this story.

Rick told me that he used to spend many hours every day reading financial publications, researching stocks, and watching the financial news. And this was after spending a long day at the office. After adopting the principles of modern portfolio theory, the efficient markets hypothesis, and passive investing, he found that he no longer needed to do those things. He recognized that he had been paying attention to what was nothing more than noise and that it only distracted him from the winner's game.

Rick and his wife sat down and calculated that by adopting a passive investment approach he had actually recaptured six weeks per year of his life! It's one thing to spend six weeks a year in productive activities. However, Rick had realized that the activities in which he was engaged were counterproductive because of the expenses and taxes incurred when he was implementing an active strategy. And, that didn't include placing a value on the most precious resource he had: time. He only had a limited amount of it and did not want to spend it on less-than-optimal activities.

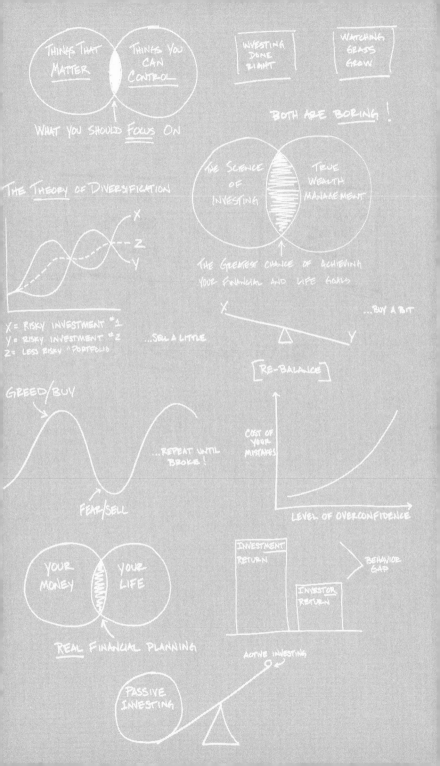

THINGS THAT MATTER

THINGS YOU CAN CONTROL

WHAT YOU SHOULD FOCUS ON

INVESTING DONE RIGHT

WATCHING GRASS GROW

BOTH ARE BORING!

THE THEORY OF DIVERSIFICATION

X

Z

Y

THE SCIENCE OF INVESTING

TRUE WEALTH MANAGEMENT

THE GREATEST CHANCE OF ACHIEVING YOUR FINANCIAL AND LIFE GOALS

X = RISKY INVESTMENT #1
Y = RISKY INVESTMENT #2
Z = LESS RISKY #PORTFOLIO

...SELL A LITTLE

X

...BUY A BIT

Y

[RE-BALANCE]

GREED/BUY

...REPEAT UNTIL BROKE!

COST OF YOUR MISTAKES

FEAR/SELL

LEVEL OF OVERCONFIDENCE

YOUR MONEY

YOUR LIFE

REAL FINANCIAL PLANNING

INVESTMENT RETURN

INVESTOR RETURN

BEHAVIOR GAP

ACTIVE INVESTING

PASSIVE INVESTING

INVESTING DONE RIGHT	WATCHING GRASS GROW

BOTH ARE BORING !

Conclusion

$\sim$

I became the director of research for BAM Advisor Services because I wanted to teach investors the knowledge necessary to make prudent investment decisions. Through my writings and interactions with investors, I believe I have accomplished that objective—though there is a lot more work to do.

The greatest pleasure I have received from my efforts is that many readers have told me that the greatest value they received from my books is that the quality of their lives has been improved. Armed with the knowledge of how markets work, and with a well-developed financial plan tailored to their unique situation, they are able to ignore the noise of the market and the investment pandering of Wall Street and focus on the "big rocks" in their lives.

I shared with you the benefits of indexing and passive investing because I feel they provide the most prudent solution for all investors. It is how you receive market returns in a low-cost and tax-efficient manner, providing you with the greatest likelihood of achieving your goals. Adopting this approach also frees you from combing through financial publications, allowing you to spend your precious free time in meaningful activities with those you love, thus enriching your life.

Finally, it is important to remember that despite what Wall Street and the financial press want you to believe, investing was never meant to be exciting. Instead, it is about achieving your financial goals with the least amount of risk. To give yourself the best chance of achieving that objective, be sure to follow my 30 Rules of Prudent Investing.

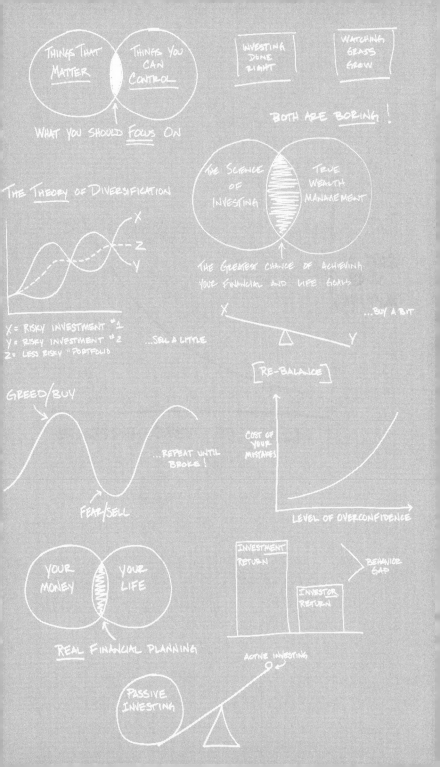

30 Rules of Prudent Investing

〜

WhIle we search for the answers to the complex problem of how to live a longer life, there are simple solutions that can have a dramatic impact. For example, it would be hard to find better advice on living longer than: do not smoke, drink alcohol in moderation, eat a balanced diet, get at least a half an hour of aerobic exercise three to four times a week, and buckle up before driving. The idea that complex problems can have simple solutions is not limited to the question of living a longer life.

I have spent almost 40 years managing financial risks for two financial institutions as well as advising individuals and multinational corporations on the management of financial risks. Based on those experiences, I have compiled a list of rules that will give you the greatest chance of achieving your financial goals:

1. **Do not take more risk than you have the ability, willingness, or need to take.** Plans fail because investors take excessive risks. The risks show up unexpectedly, which leads to the abandonment of plans. When developing your plan, consider your horizon, stability of income, ability to tolerate losses, and the rate of return required to meet your goals.

2. **Never invest in any security unless you fully understand the nature of all of the risks**. If you cannot explain the risks to your friends, you should not invest. Fortunes have been lost because people did not understand the type of risks they were taking.

3. **The more complex the investment, the faster you should run away**. Complex products are designed to be sold, not bought. You can be sure the complexity is designed in favor of the issuer, not the investor. Investment bankers do not play Santa Claus and hand over higher returns because they like you.

4. **Risk and return are not necessarily related; risk and *expected* return are related**. If there were

no risk, there would not be higher expected returns.

5. **If the security has a high yield, you can be sure the risks are high even if you cannot see them**. The high yield is like the shiny apple with which the evil queen entices Snow White. Investors should never confuse yield with expected return. Snow White could not see the poison inside the apple. Similarly, investment risks may be hidden, but you can be sure they are there.

6. **A well-designed plan is necessary for successful investing, but you must also have the discipline to stay the course, rebalance, and tax-manage as needed**. Unfortunately, most investors have no written plan. And emotions such as greed and envy in bull markets and fear and panic in bear markets can cause even well-designed plans to be discarded.

7. **Investment plans must be integrated into well-designed estate, tax, and risk-management (insurance of all kinds) plans**. The best investment plans can fail because of events unrelated

to financial markets. For example, the bread-winner dies without sufficient life insurance or suffers an accident and has insufficient liability, disability, or long-term-care insurance in place.

8. **Do not treat the highly improbable as impossible or the highly likely as certain**. Investors assume that if their horizon is long enough, there is little to no risk. The result is they take too much risk. Taking too much risk causes investors with long horizons to become short-term investors. Stocks are risky no matter the horizon. And remember, just because something has not happened, doesn't mean it cannot or will not.

9. **The consequences of decisions should dominate the probability of outcomes**. We buy insurance against low-probability events (such as death) when the consequences of not having the insurance can be too great. Similarly, investors should insure their portfolios (by having an appropriate amount of high-quality bonds) against low-probability events when the consequences of not doing so can be too great to even contemplate, let alone accept.

10. **The strategy to get rich is entirely different from the strategy to stay rich.** One gets rich by taking risks (or inheriting the assets). One stays rich by minimizing risks, diversifying, and not spending too much.

11. **The only thing worse than having to pay taxes is not having to pay them**. The "too-many-eggs-in-one-basket" problem often results from holding a large amount of stock with a low cost basis. Large fortunes have been lost because of the refusal to pay taxes.

12. **The safest port in a sea of uncertainty is diversification**. Portfolios should include appropriate allocations to the asset classes of large-cap and small-cap, value and growth, real estate, international developed markets, emerging markets, commodities, and bonds.

13. **Diversification is always working; sometimes you'll like the results and sometimes you won't.** Once you diversify beyond popular indexes (such as the S&P 500), you will be faced with periods when a popular benchmark index outperforms your portfolio. The noise of the

media will test your ability to adhere to your strategy.

14. **The prices of all stock and risky bond assets (such as high-yield bonds and emerging market bonds) tend to fall during financial crises**. Your plan must account for this.

15. **It isn't enough to find mispriced securities. You have to make money after accounting for the costs**. The "history books" are filled with investors who tried to exploit "mispricings," only to find that the costs exceeded any benefits.

16. **Stock investing is a positive sum game; expenses make outperforming the market a negative sum game**. Risk-averse investors do not play negative sum games. And most investors are risk averse. Use only low-cost, tax-efficient, and passively managed investments.

17. **Owning individual stocks and sector funds is more akin to speculating than investing**. The market compensates investors for risks that cannot be diversified away, like the risk of investing in stocks versus bonds. Investors shouldn't expect compensation for diversifiable risk—

the unique risks related to owning one stock. Prudent investors accept risk only for situations in which they will be compensated with higher expected returns.

18. **Take your risks with stocks**. The role of bonds is to provide the anchor to the portfolio, reducing overall portfolio risk to the appropriate level.

19. **Before acting on seemingly valuable information, ask yourself why you believe that information is not already incorporated into prices**. Only *incremental* insight has value. Capturing *incremental* insight is difficult because there are so many smart, highly motivated analysts doing the same research. If you hear recommendations on CNBC, from your broker, or read them in *Barron's*, the market already knows the information it is based on. It has already been incorporated into prices and has no value.

20. **The five most dangerous investment words are "This time, it is different."** Getting caught up in the mania of the "new thing" is why "the surest way to create a small fortune is to start out with a large one" is a cliché.

21. **The market can remain irrational longer than you can remain solvent**. Bubbles do occur. However, while they eventually burst, they can grow larger and last longer than your resources.

22. **If it sounds too good to be true, it is.** When money meets experience, the experience gets the money and the money gets the experience. The only free lunch in investing is diversification.

23. **Never work with a commission-based investment advisor.** Commissions create the potential for biased advice.

24. **Only work with advisors who will provide a fiduciary standard of care**. That is the best way to be sure the advice provided is in your best interest. There is no reason not to insist on a fiduciary standard.

25. **Separate the services of financial advisor, money managers, custodian, and trustee**. This minimizes the risk of fraud.

26. **Since we live in a world of cloudy crystal balls, a strategy is either right or wrong before we**

know the outcome. In general, lucky fools do not have any idea they are lucky. Even well-designed plans can fail, because risks that were accepted occur. And risks that were avoided because the consequences of their materializing would be too great to accept may not occur.

27. **Hope is not an investment strategy**. Base your decisions on the evidence from peer-reviewed academic journals.

28. **Keep a diary of your predictions about the market**. After a while, you will conclude that you should not act on your "insights."

29. **There is nothing new in investing, just the investment history you do not know**. The knowledge of financial history will enable you to anticipate risks and incorporate them into your plan.

30. **Good advice does not have to be expensive; but bad advice always costs you dearly, no matter how little you pay for it**. Smart people do not choose the cheapest doctor or the cheapest CPA. Costs matter, but it is the value added relative to the cost of the advice that ultimately is most important.

The following is not only the most important message in the book, but is a fitting ending. While it is a tragedy that the vast majority of investors unnecessarily miss out on market returns that are available to anyone adopting a passive investment strategy, the truly great tragedy is that they also miss out on the important things in life in pursuit of what I call the "Holy Grail of Outperformance." My fondest wish is that this book has led you to the winner's game in both investing and, far more important, life.

Notes

Chapter One

1. 1993 *Berkshire Hathaway Annual Report.*
2. 1996 *Berkshire Hathaway Annual Report.*
3. 2004 *Berkshire Hathaway Annual Report.*
4. Ibid.
5. James Altucher, *Trade Like Warren Buffett* (New York: Wiley, 2005).
6. Mark Sellers, "Could Stocks Still Be Undervalued?" February 18, 2004, http://news.morningstar.com /articlenet/article.aspx?id=104110
7. *Newsweek,* August 7, 1995.
8. William Sherden, *The Fortune Sellers* (New York: Wiley, 1998).
9. Ibid.
10. Ibid.
11. Philip E. Tetlock, *Expert Political Judgment* (Princeton, NJ: Princeton University Press, 2006).
12. Carl Richards, *The Behavior Gap* (New York: Penguin, 2012).
13. 1988 *Berkshire Hathaway Annual Report.*
14. 1991 *Berkshire Hathaway Annual Report.*
15. *BusinessWeek,* June 25, 1995.
16. 1996 *Berkshire Hathaway Annual Report.*

17. Dan Kadlec, "Warren Buffett Is Buying. Is It Time to Celebrate?" *Time,* November 09, 2011, http://money land.time.com/2011/11/09/warren-buffett-is-buying -is-it-time-to-celebrate/
18. 2008 *Berkshire Hathaway Chairman's Letter.*
19. 1990 *Berkshire Hathaway Chairman's Letter.*

Chapter Two

1. Floyd Norris, "The Upside? Things Could Be Worse," *New York Times,* December 23, 2010, http://www.nytimes .com/2010/12/24/business/24norris.html?ref =business
2. Adam's Smith's "Money World" show, June 20, 1988, http://www.lestout.com/article/business/business -news/warren-buffet-advice-during-a-crisis.html
3. Clifford Asness, "Rubble Logic: What Did We Learn From the Great Stock Market Bubble?," *Financial Analysts Journal,* November/December 2005.
4. http://www.buffettcup.com/Default.aspx?tabid=69
5. *BusinessWeek,* June 25, 1999.

Chapter Three

1. Brad Barber and Terrance Odean, "Boys Will Be Boys: Gender, Overconfidence and Common Stock Investment, *Quarterly Journal of Economics,* February 2001.
2. Ibid.
3. Brad Barber and Terrance Odean, "Do Investors Trade Too Much?" *American Economic Review,* December 1999.
4. Ibid.
5. Wilber G. Lewellen, Ronald C. Lease, and Gary G. Schlarbaum, "Patterns of Investor Strategy and Behavior Among Individual Investors," *Journal of Business,* 50 1977, pp. 296–333.
6. Ibid.

7. Brad Barber and Terrance Odean, "Too Many Cooks Spoil the Profits," *Financial Analysts Journal*, January/February 2000.

8. *Smart Money*, June 2001.

9. Markus Glaser and Martin Weber, "Why Inexperienced Investors Do Not Learn: They Don't Know Their Past Portfolio Performance," July 2007.

10. Mark Carhart, "On Persistence in Mutual-fund Performance," *Journal of Finance*, March 1997.

11. Ibid.

12. Ibid.

13. Russel Kinnel, "How Expense Ratios and Star Ratings Predict Success," *Morningstar Advisor*, August 10, 2010.

14. Jonathan B. Berk, "Five Myths of Active Management."

15. 1993 *Berkshire Hathaway Annual Report*.

16. Amit Goyal and Sunil Wahal, "The Selection and Termination of Investment Management Firms by Plan Sponsors," May 2005.

17. Edwin J. Elton, Martin J. Gruber, and Christopher R. Blake, "Participant Reaction and the Performance of Funds Offered by 401(k) Plans," *Journal of Financial Intermediation*, May 2006.

18. William Sharpe, "The Arithmetic of Active Management," *The Financial Analysts Journal*, January/February 1991, pp. 7–9.

Sources

The following are the sources for data contained in the text:

Standard & Poor's for data on the S&P 500 Index and the S&P GSCI. Used with permission.

Kenneth R. French and the Center for Research in Security Prices at the University of Chicago for data on the various Fama-French series. Used with permission.

Morgan Stanley for data on the MSCI indexes. www.msci.com Used with permission.

Barclays for data on the Barclays Capital Intermediate Government/Credit Index. Used with permission.

Index

Acknowledgments

For all their support and encouragement, I would like to thank the principals of BAM Advisor Services: Adam Birenbaum, Ernest Clark, Madaline Creehan, Thelia Eagan, Bob Gellman, Ed Goldberg, Joe Goldberg, Mont Levy, Vladimir Masek, Al Sears, Bert Schweizer III, Brent Thomas and Brenda Witt.

Thanks also go to those who read early drafts of this book and made significant contributions: Wendy Cook, Eric Ess, Mike Going, Kevin Grogan, Jo-Ann Gallerstein, Matt Hall, Stephen High, Scott Lucia, and Alex Madlener.

And a special thanks to Carl Richards for putting my vision to paper on the illustration in Chapter 8, as well as providing the other illustrations.

RC Balaban is the editor of my blog at CBSNews .com, as well as the co-author of *Investment Mistakes Even Smart Investors Make.* If you enjoyed this book, RC deserves much of the credit. The usual caveat of any errors being my own certainly applies.

I also thank my agent Sam Fleischman for all his efforts over the years and for getting me started as an author. I am forever grateful for his support and friendship.

I especially thank my wife, Mona, the love of my life. Walking through life with her has truly been a gracious experience.

About the Author

 **Larry E. Swedroe** is a principal and the Director of Research for the BAM Alliance. He has also held executive-level positions at Prudential Home Mortgage, Citicorp, and CBS. Swedroe frequently speaks at financial conferences throughout the year and writes the blog Wise Investing at CBSNews.com.